WORKTOWN
The Drawings of Falcon Hildred

WORKTOWN
The Drawings of Falcon Hildred

Peter Wakelin

Foreword by Sir Neil Cossons

Comisiwn Brenhinol Henebion Cymru
Royal Commission
on the Ancient and Historical Monuments of Wales

In association with the Ironbridge Gorge Museum Trust

ROYAL COMMISSIONERS

Chairman:
Dr Eurwyn Wiliam MA, PhD, FSA

Vice Chairman:
Mr Henry Owen-John BA, MIFA, FSA

Mrs Anne S. Eastham BA, FSA
Ms Catherine Hardman BA, MA
Mr Jonathan Mathews Hudson MBCS, CITP
Mr Thomas Lloyd OBE, MA, FSA, DL
Dr Mark Redknap BA, PhD, MIFA, FSA
Professor C. M. Williams BA, PhD, FRHistS

Secretary:
Dr Peter Wakelin BA, MSocSc, PhD, FSA

ISBN 978-1-871184-47-1

British Library Cataloguing in Publication Data.
A catalogue record for this book is available from the British Library.

© Crown Copyright. RCAHMW 2012. All rights reserved.

No part of this book may be reproduced, stored in a retrieval system or transmitted in any form or by any means, electronic, mechanical, photocopying, recording, scanning or otherwise, without permission from the publisher:

Comisiwn Brenhinol Henebion Cymru
Royal Commission
on the Ancient and Historical Monuments of Wales

Crown Building, Plas Crug, Aberystwyth, Ceredigion, SY23 1NJ

Telephone: 01970 621200, email - nmr.wales@rcahmw.gov.uk
Website: www.rcahmw.gov.uk

Half-title page: *Pasture Street Panorama*, 1987

This panorama shows the house where Falcon Hildred was born, on the left, and was reconstructed from a series of photographs.

Pencil. ink and watercolour on paper, 75 x 35 cm. FHA 03/01

Opposite title page: *Park Street shop, Coventry, 1978*

This uncharacteristically colourful image captures a boarded-up shop in Coventry, typical of the many small, humble buildings that were once at the centre of communities but have since disappeared from the landscape.

Acrylic on paper, 13 x 14 cm. FHA 03/21

The Falcon Hildred Access and Learning Project

The Royal Commission on the Ancient and Historical Monuments of Wales, working in partnership with the Ironbridge Gorge Museum Trust and with support from the Heritage Lottery Fund, has acquired a unique collection of over 600 original drawings of industrial buildings and landscapes by the artist Falcon Hildred.

Falcon Hildred has dedicated his working life to recording the buildings and landscapes of nineteenth-and twentieth-century industry, producing works of high aesthetic, historical and social value. He has recorded in detail technological and engineering change and a rapidly disappearing way of life.

The Falcon Hildred Access and Learning Project preserves this valuable resource for the enjoyment of future generations, and opens access to the collection through a coordinated programme of digitisation, exhibition and education across England and Wales. The collection can be accessed at the Royal Commission's offices in Aberystwyth, or online at:
www.coflein.gov.uk and www.peoplescollectionwales.co.uk.
Digital copies of the images are also available to view at Ironbridge Gorge Museum.

All images in this book are Crown Copyright © Royal Commission on the Ancient and Historical Monuments of Wales: Falcon Hildred Collection, with the exceptions of:

Falcon Hildred, reproduced with permission of Newport Museum and Art Gallery, pages 69, 70, 71, 72, 73, 96, 97, 98, 112, 113, 114, 115, 122, 138, 139, 140, 141, 163

Falcon Hildred, courtesy of the Ironbridge Gorge Museum Trust, pages 5, 68, 126

Clive Hicks-Jenkins, page 24; Sally Wakelin, page 24;
The Piper Estate, page 46; Joan Isaac, page 47

Opposite: *Menai Bridge*, 1981

One of a series of sketches of Menai Bridge in Anglesey, commissioned by the Ironbridge Gorge Museum Trust.

Pencil and watercolour on paper, 18.5 x 11 cm. FHA 2011.784
The Ironbridge Gorge Museum Trust, Telford Collection:
IGMT.2011.784 - NPRN 268065

Contents

Foreword - Sir Neil Cossons - 7

Falcon Hildred and the Art of Recording - 9

Townscapes - 51

Housing - 75

Public and Commercial Buildings - 99

Churches and Chapels - 117

Transport and Engineering - 127

Industrial Buildings - 143

The Landscape of Slate - 165

Rural Life and Industry - 183

My Working Process – Falcon Hildred - 193

Finding out more - 198

Notes - 199

Acknowledgements - 199

Index - 200

FDH '76

Foreword by Sir Neil Cossons

Falcon Hildred has made one of the most distinctive and distinguished of contributions to the iconography of the Industrial Revolution. Captivated by the soul and spirit of discarded working places, his insights, portrayed over a lifetime of subtle and discerning observation, offer a thoughtful and often moving perspective on a disappeared and unacknowledged past. The artist's eye is easily deluded, seduced by fashion or constrained by convention. But in Falcon Hildred the overwhelming power of the ordinary and his capacity to evoke its qualities have enabled him to offer his own very personal view of the life and meanings that still cling to these landscapes of abandonment. Through his keenly perceived illustrations we are no longer trespassers in these elusive places.

Falcon Hildred grew up in Grimsby, his boyhood intensely coloured by a town that in the 1950s laid convincing claim to being the world's largest fishing port. But he also witnessed at first hand the virtual extinction of the industry that for a century had dominated the town, and saw the decline and dereliction that resulted. Here lie the roots of his passion, for places that were once but are no more, that inhabit the transient, unoccupied tenancy between yesterday and tomorrow. Today, he lives in Blaenau Ffestiniog, at the heart of the north Wales slate industry. But, unlike Grimsby, Blaenau offers a sanctuary where change verges on the timeless and the past can still be savoured and understood as part of the present.

I first became aware of Falcon's work in the mid-1970s, enthralled by his refined and understated style, his draughtsmanship, and his ability to capture and portray qualities that for many people would be invisible – the serene Victorian confidence of 111 Prospect Vale in south-east London; the melancholy of Hertford Square, Coventry, where demolition exposes, almost obscenely, the white-painted interior of the top-floor weaver's shop; the virtuoso extravagance of Cash's 1857 chimney, drawn as if by its architect but softened by a century's patina. To live with these pictures has been a joy and a reminder in a cacophonous world of how important it is to chronicle the quiet, the unseen and the commonplace.

Falcon Hildred maintains such a secure foothold in the working past because he is of a generation who remembers when it was the present. There were no signposts to the world he portrays, but through his works, now permanently secured, and this book, we can be the beneficiaries of his discriminating eye and sense of judgement.

Neil Cossons

Rushbury, Shropshire
August 2012

Evening traffic crossing Byker Bridge, 1976

The elegant Byker toll bridge was opened in 1879, flying across the Ouseburn valley in Newcastle upon Tyne. Behind it in this view along Lime Street is the Ouseburn railway viaduct of 1839, the original timber spans of which were replaced in 1869 with the delicate ironwork silhouetted in the drawing. Both bridges, the chimney and the Ship Inn between them have become local icons, but the area is no longer the industrial one portrayed in 1976 and specialises instead in arts and heritage.

Chalk on paper, 13 x 16 cm. FHA 03/43

Falcon Hildred in his drawing office, Melin Pant-yr-ynn
Photograph: Iain Wright, Royal Commission, 2011
DS2011_342_027

Falcon Hildred and the Art of Recording

Since the late 1950s, Falcon Hildred's lifelong mission has been to make a visual record of disappearing buildings that stood for an industrial culture itself threatened with extinction. He began because he saw whole landscapes of factories, mines, workers' houses and communities being swept away. In many areas, old industries were collapsing, long-established communities were being replaced by mass rehousing schemes and ambitious urban redevelopment was beginning to take hold. Elsewhere, the forces of nature or a demand for tidiness were causing familiar ruins to vanish from sight forever. Falcon could do little to halt this march, but as a skilled designer and illustrator there was one thing he could achieve: he could ensure that monuments to the past did not disappear without some record being made.

During the past half century Falcon has documented a wealth of urban and industrial buildings and landscapes through accurate, detailed and evocative drawings. This book aims to discuss and demonstrate his achievement in interpreting for future generations the culture of the industrial era in Britain. He was motivated by a sense that buildings could hold up a mirror to the lives of the people who had built, used and inhabited them. He said in an interview in 2011:

> *The thing about buildings is that they're about people. [...] Everything we do in life is either in or around buildings. We celebrate, we teach, we live, we work, we heal, we compete, we store – everything is done in and around buildings, and they therefore embody all our needs, all our hopes, our beliefs, our fears. They are the symbols of all our values, really, in civilisation, from cottage to cathedral. They are the symbols of what we want and what we believe. So the risk is that when you destroy a building you risk destroying something of ourselves.*[1]

His instinct that something of real importance was being lost was soon reinforced by learning about the pivotal historical importance of industrial Britain. As he says, commerce and industry 'achieved more in two centuries to transform and improve the lives of every ordinary person than everything throughout our entire history.' For Falcon, this realisation brought a commitment to making his records not just visually satisfying, but accurate and informative enough to preserve for future generations the value of the original artefacts as evidence of the past.

He began to see recording as an act of paying respect to people who had spent their lives creating wealth, bringing material improvements to living standards or fighting for rights and

---

Pant-yr-ynn Mill, end view from the south, 1999.

Falcon Hildred's home since 1969, a water-powered former slate mill at Bethania, Blaenau Ffestiniog, sits in a landscape of work, with slate quarry tips breaking the horizon above and terraced houses below.

Ink and watercolour on paper, 16 x 14 cm. FHA 01/191 - NPRN 28620

Demolition of Penygroes, 1982

A frequent scene throughout Falcon's lifetime of documenting buildings at risk has been that of demolition in progress. This terrace of slate workers' houses was just below Pant-yr-ynn mill in Bethania. He was too late to make a detailed record, but captured this emotive scene of destruction under street lights one winter night.

Felt pen and watercolour, 24 x 36 cm.   FHA 01/098, NPRN 305760

---

opportunities, whether through industry, home life or social and political campaigning. When he dismantled a fireplace from a Blaenau Ffestiniog slate quarryman's cottage before it was demolished, and installed it in his mill, he hung above it a photograph of the quarryman, Tommy Owen. He produced a note for visitors to read that expressed his feelings about this one man and what he stood for:

There was nothing special about Tommy. And that's the whole point. He was just one of millions of ordinary working men, women and at one time even children who toiled all their lives in mines and mills, or who hauled, stitched, laid bricks, riveted, farmed the land or fished the perilous seas; managed the home, mended and made do, went hungry and without, endured and eventually agitated and in many cases even died to bring about the easy life we now enjoy yet take so much for granted.

If Falcon's lifetime's worth of drawings stand as tributes to the achievements of people of the past, they also represent something else that Falcon sees as a precious human quality: craftsmanship and care. For him, many of the buildings he was recording, however humble, were products of a mindful, intimately scaled and personal way of making our surroundings; a closeness of maker to product that is far less in evidence in the twenty-first century. He talks with enthusiasm of hand-thrown ceramic chimney pots, simple flourishes that were part of the design of brass taps or the thoughtful choice of patterned ridge tiles to finish off a roof. He points out that often there was no requirement for an object, building or engineering work to be good to look at yet it acquired beauty because it was a work of personal skill, created by hand and eye rather than by bulldozer or machine. Buildings need not be works of architecture to

Drum-house to Rhiw-bach quarry, 1981

The site sketch, dated 23 March 1981, shows the drum-house at the top of the second incline taking slate trams to and from Rhiw-bach quarry. It is an example of the use of slate waste to build sturdy structures. Falcon was anxious to record buildings like this that are so characteristic of the slate landscapes of north Wales before they were lost to nature after decades of disuse.

Pencil and watercolour on paper, 19 x 27 cm.
FHA 01/186/02 - NPRN 40568

---

be beautiful; the slate mining landscape around his home in Blaenau Ffestiniog is rich in constructions of slate rubble that embody unexpected refinement. He explained in an interview in 2011,

> You look at a drum-house or some stonework and it's been placed with care. Even the rubbish that has been moved, it's been compactly placed; it's not just been moved with brute force, it's been moved with intelligence and economy and skill, and even with pride because when they built a drum-house or any building the masonry is very attractive, even though it's very functional and even though it's only waste. It's still got pride. Well, that's human, isn't it?

Capturing the fine detail is always of importance for Falcon because it shows the hand of the human being at work. His drawing of the corrugated-iron premises in Blaenau Ffestiniog of 'R. L. Jones and Son, Builders and Undertakers' shows the personality of a pair of buildings that have been created, used and moulded by successive people to fit the way they lived and worked – becoming the centre of someone's world. When corrugated iron was a high-tech new material, these premises might have been designed to show off its convenience and versatility, but they have lasted for generations during which corrugated iron has spiralled downward in esteem (though it is now appreciated by some for its rarity, age and patina). Look closely at a building like this, and at Falcon's record of it, and you see the lives lived with it – the steps worn by working boots, the stovepipe put through the roof to give a bit of warmth, the doors inserted to make access for the changing needs of building materials and coffins.

The drawings in this book have been made over a period of fifty

Builder and undertaker, 1978

The corrugated-iron buildings of R. L. Jones and Son, Blaenau Ffestiniog, sketched on site in June 1978.

Pencil and watercolour on paper, 21 x 28 cm.   FHA 01/126 - NPRN 410597

---

years. During that time, the vast majority of the buildings and townscapes that Falcon judged to be at risk have indeed disappeared or else changed beyond all recognition. The corrugated-iron workshop of Jones and Son seemed one of the most vulnerable when Falcon drew it in 1978, but ironically it is among relatively few that (as yet) remain intact, underlining the happenstance that decides what survives from our past and what does not.

Falcon's working life has been an odyssey travelled through places where he saw work that needed to be done in recording and celebrating threatened built heritage. He has been especially thorough in his account of Blaenau Ffestiniog, his home since 1969, where he has been on hand, watching the decay of disused quarries and the demolition of houses, community buildings and commercial premises. Other places whose buildings and landscapes figure strongly in his life's work are London, where he began recording, his home towns of Grimsby and Coventry, and other cities where he has chosen to work such as Cardiff and Newcastle upon Tyne. Newport is well represented by a set of drawings commissioned from him by Newport Museum and Art Gallery.

Though his greatest focus has been on the legacy of nineteenth-century industrial communities, his subjects have ranged widely within this frame, as indicated by the chapters of this book: they extend from townscapes, housing, public buildings of many kinds and churches and chapels, to transport and engineering works, industrial buildings and landscapes of the slate industry, as well as a miscellany of other buildings that have caught his eye.

Falcon David Hildred was born in the east-coast fishing port of Grimsby in 1935. He spent his earliest years there and along the Lincolnshire coast in Cleethorpes. His surname is a common one in the region, but he was given his unusual first name probably after the Antarctic explorer Captain Robert Falcon Scott. He says, 'My parents had the kindness and good sense to use my middle name, David, while I went through school, but by the time I reached the age of seventeen [in the more liberal environment of an art college], I was happy to give Falcon a try.'[2]

He was always drawing as an infant, showing a talent for it like his father and his older brother Arthur. His father had never had a chance to pursue his love of art, a working-class man whose opportunities were deflected by two world wars and the intervening Great Depression. Falcon remembers his own interest in buildings starting at the age of about five. It was about then that the family took a trip on the ferry across the Humber estuary to Hull and Falcon was inspired by the vast commercial and industrial buildings of the port, so much larger and more impressive than anything he had seen before. He came home perceiving everything in a new way. From this early age, he recalls that he was attracted not so much by fine architecture as by 'our immediate environment'.

We lived in a typical terrace house which backed onto a factory producing jams and preserves and had 'Tickler's' painted in big letters down the chimney. Beyond that was the railway with a goods yard and a level-crossing, and beyond that, Hewitt's brewery. To the left was the gasworks and a little distance away to the right were the fish docks with their smokehouses. And of course it was still the great days of railways, so there was the constant sound of steam trains and the level-crossing bell; and at tide-time the sound of ships' sirens. It was a world inhabited by the sounds, shapes and smells of industry. And of course it never stopped. All day and throughout the night work went on. But it was never noisy, just there in the background, a gentle, soothing rhythm, reassuring. I would lie in my bed waiting to catch the sounds of the little shunting engines marshalling wagons – chuff chuff chuff, the little whistle – and every so often the gasworks would sigh as though pausing in its labours. That was my lullaby.[3]

Pasture Street crossing, Grimsby, 1978
This picture, based on observations in 1953 and drawn in 1978, captures Falcon's memories of the railway crossing near the house where as a child he was lulled to sleep by the sound of shunting.
Pencil and watercolour on paper, 13.5 x 17 cm. FHA 03/62

One of his early inspirations was the family's book of drawings of Chester by Joseph Pike (1883-1956), an illustrator who specialised in architectural subjects and produced four published 'sketchbooks': of Chester, Cardiff, Bruges and Ampleforth College. Falcon admired the intricacy and accuracy with which Pike captured the personality of the buildings. He realises looking back that he was influenced especially by the way in which Pike drew vignettes – focussing on the subject of interest and letting the image dissolve into white paper around it. He notes, 'I very rarely

Chester: A Sketchbook by Joseph Pike, published by A & C Black in 1920 and republished by them in 2009. Falcon grew up with a copy of the book in his home and was fascinated by the detailed vignettes of historic buildings.

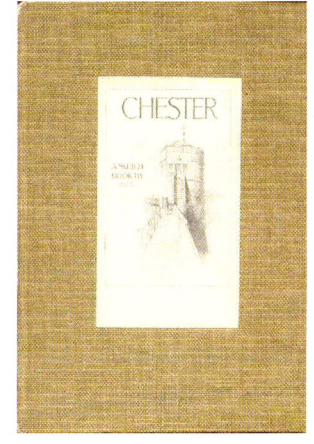

FCH.38/76

draw to the edge of the paper; I just draw what I think is important, then stop.'

As the war began, Lincolnshire was at risk of bombing and even of invasion. When Falcon's father and older sister Trevlynn were both posted to an aircraft factory in Coventry it was decided that the whole family would relocate. The Coventry Blitz had already taken place, in November 1940, and they found themselves arriving in a devastated city and a bomb-damaged home. Falcon could hardly fail to be affected as he grew up to learn about the destruction of the buildings of a great medieval city as well as the terrible loss of life. Coventry cathedral had become a beacon of defiance against the Nazi leadership's 'Baedeker Raid' strategy to attack Britain's culture along with its military resolve: the cathedral's great apse stood amid the destruction like a frail but enduring bastion and the artist John Piper's vivid image of it, painted the morning after the eleven-hour bombing raid that devastated the cathedral, had been issued as a postcard by the Ministry of Information.

Falcon failed his eleven-plus exam, missing the opportunity to go to grammar school. But at age thirteen he succeeded in getting a place in Coventry art school's junior department. This took in girls as well as boys and was situated in a small and attractive Edwardian villa – all very different from the sprawling, all-boys secondary school he had been attending. Given his aptitudes and temperament it was a perfect education. Half the work was art, the other half was studying subjects partly through visual means – the students were issued with exercise books with lined paper on one side for writing and blank paper on the other for drawing. He recalls learning about history from the Prehistoric to the industrial period and going out drawing buildings around Coventry as part of his studies. This was his initiation into observing the destruction of buildings and a first prompt to what would become his passion to record them. He learned through a process of looking hard at such evidence in his surroundings. He says, 'Drawing really makes you look. [...] You have to understand what you're drawing.'

He moved on through the intermediate and then the senior arts departments at Coventry. He recalls studying lettering, life drawing, pictorial composition, printing: 'We did everything and I loved it all.' The college principal, Mr Hoskin, involved his students in real projects he was working on, such as preparing for arts balls or

Photograph of a rocking chair, 1965

This photograph shows a prototype of a rocking chair designed and made by Falcon Hildred while he was at the Royal College of Art. A small batch of the chairs was made and sold at furniture stores, including Heals.

FHA 07/13/02

On the dole, Grimsby, 1976

Falcon recorded a memory of the street where he grew up in Grimsby in this drawing which he dated 1938/1976. He wrote underneath it, 'One day in the late thirties when I was very small, a man came and played a cornet in our street. Falling rain and his lament were the only sounds. As we drew near, my father explained about being out of work, and got me to run over and give him some money. I can still remember the feeling of desolation.'

Pencil on paper, 15 x 17 cm. FHA 03/53

building a giant model of the cathedral as a Christmas decoration for the devastated city centre. In another project, Falcon made studies of styles of architecture, producing sheets of illustrations to characterise each era – one reconstructed Coventry cathedral as an archetype of the Perpendicular style, after it had been decided to build a modern cathedral next to the medieval fragments. While he would have loved to be an architect himself, he realised he lacked the necessary abilities in maths and physics. But he knew he could be a designer. As a result, he chose to study industrial design at Birmingham college of art, working with wood, metal and plastics and designing and making furniture.

After Birmingham and two years' national service, Falcon won a

Perpendicular architecture, 1954

An architectural history sheet drawn as a student at Birmingham college of art to show the Perpendicular style, referencing the old Coventry cathedral, which had been largely destroyed by bombing and was eventually to be replaced by Sir Basil Spence's new cathedral alongside the ruin. Falcon noted under his main perspective of the building, 'restored', and focused his attention on the apsidal end, which survived as a skeletal symbol of the city's wartime suffering. The drawing bears the tutor's mark, 10 out of 10, and it remains the artist's favourite of his student drawings.

Ink and sepia wash on paper, 58 x 40 cm. FHA 06/03

DETAIL OF SOUTH CHAPEL SCREEN, ST JOHN'S COVENTRY

WASHING PLACE, NORTH CLOISTER GLOUSTER CATHEDRAL

DOOR ST JOHN'S COVENTRY

CAPITAL ON THE OAK LECTERN OF ST JOHN'S COVENTRY

COVENTRY CATHEDRAL (RESTORED)

CAPPERS CHAPEL · CHAPEL OF THE RESURRECTION · SMITHS CHAPEL · DYERS CHAPEL · STEEPLE

PERPENDICULAR ARCHITECTURE

FALCON HILDRED · 6 MARCH 54 · Nº 25

Perspective drawing of furniture, 1955

One of Falcon Hildred's designs as a student for library furniture at Coventry college of art, showing the post-war enthusiasm for lightness and colour and the influences of Scandinavian design and the Festival of Britain.

Pencil and watercolour on paper, 58 x 40 cm. FHA 06/08/02

place for three years at the hothouse for artistic and design talent that was the Royal College of Art in South Kensington. He won a medal for work of distinction. This led to what he describes as 'a lovely job' with a firm of architects in London, Ward and Austin, specialising in ships' interiors. He designed cabins, lounges, bars and furniture for cargo vessels and ferries. He enjoyed the work enormously and his surviving drawings of the time show his sympathy for the optimism of the radically clean-lined modernist styles of the period. They also show his facility for making accurate drawings that would enable the objects to be created, a skill that would later inform his thorough documentation of buildings at risk.

However, Falcon became more and more aware of how quickly the industrial culture he had grown up amidst was being destroyed. He realised he would have to find some way of focusing his time on recording, perhaps leaving this golden period of employment behind him. Throughout the early and mid 1960s, he had been keen to be part of the post-war rebuilding, bringing good design and fresh colour to Britain after the restrictions of the Great Depression and wartime. Nevertheless, he could see that in many cases this process also meant clearing away the built environments of the past. He started to notice the speed of change in London's boroughs, where the march of post-war progress in demolishing nineteenth-century housing developments was at least as fast as it was in the declining

Design for a first-class bar on a ship, 1965

Watercolour, ink and candle wax on paper, 59 x 42 cm. FHA 07/05

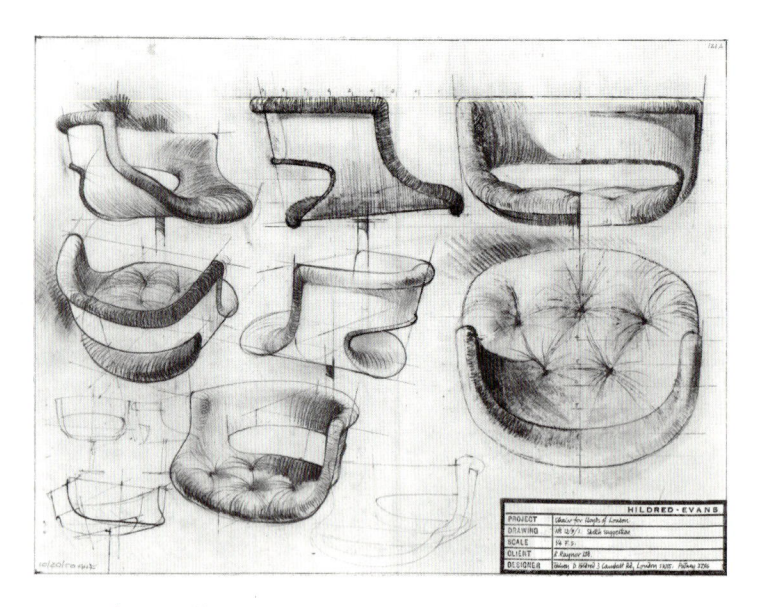

Design for an office chair, 1966

This is one of the first designs made for the Hildred-Evans industrial design partnership that provided Falcon with some of his commercial work in the late 1960s and 1970s. The drawing shows all perspectives of the chair. The client was R. Rayner Ltd, for Lloyds of London.

Pencil on paper, 42 x 30 cm. FHA 07/03/01

Design drawing for a ship's cabin, 1965

The sleek, modern design of this cabin would not look out of place in a twenty-first century hotel.

Ink, wax and watercolour on paper, 59 x 42 cm. FHA 07/04/02

industrial centres of the midlands. He began making drawings that captured the tidy houses of Woolwich and the huddled and irregular backs of terraces in Lansdowne Lane, Charlton.

One London drawing of this time is interesting for quite different reasons: it captured the interior of Falcon's flat in Putney as a souvenir for his mother after a visit. Showing a bed-sitting room at the front and a dedicated workroom at the back, it suggests a life increasingly focused around the drawing board where he would work on his recording after leaving the office.

Falcon returned regularly to see his family in Coventry and while there he heard about the plans for comprehensive redevelopment after the devastation of the war. The plans reached far beyond the bomb-damaged properties and extended to the demolition of whole areas. As they began to be implemented he saw the market hall tower go, warehouses pulled down and, as in London, terraced houses cleared for high-rise living. He realised he couldn't stand by while so much of his home town disappeared, so he started to return to Coventry at weekends to survey buildings and draw up accurate records of them. What upset him most was when he saw what he considered to be good buildings reduced to rubble. He found himself rushing to keep up with the destruction and sketched many even as demolition was in progress.

One weekend when Falcon and his friend Rita had decided to give themselves a rare break away from recording they came back through the area of Coventry they had intended to study next. They were shocked to discover everything had been destroyed already. The buildings had been built cheaply, and they had come down quickly and easily. They might not have been architecture of high quality but they had been the centre of communities for generations and embodied thousands of life stories. Falcon was so devastated that he straight away went to see his employer, Neville Ward, and told him that he felt he must leave the firm to devote himself to recording. To his astonishment, Mr Ward generously offered to keep him on half time so that he could have a partial salary as a safety net while he started out on his own. This was agreed, and Falcon began in earnest what would be his lifetime's work.

Having more time for his projects brought changes in Falcon's working practices. He found he was able to select buildings to record in a more orderly way rather than merely keep up with the demolition teams. He also found that he at last had time to work up drawings based on his much earlier site-sketches and field notes – this explains why many finished drawings have two dates on them, the date observed and the date completed, and why many were worked up years after the buildings had been demolished. Sketches made on site remained fundamental to his work, however (usually identified by an 'S' after the date). He still judges that drawing directly in front of the subject is the most efficient and accurate way of capturing information. The sketches he continues to make on site, though they may be sometimes blotched by rain or torn by the wind, have a vitality and immediacy that viewers find appealing.

In due course, Falcon gave up his part-time job, too, so as to draw buildings in as much of his time as possible. He earned money instead through teaching and occasional design projects. He established Hildred-Evans Industrial Design Consultants with Gareth J. Evans to design both buildings and furniture, based initially at his flat in Putney. But in order to reduce his living expenses he started looking for somewhere to live outside London.

Since his childhood in the flat lands of Lincolnshire, Falcon had been fascinated by rocks and hills. Towards the end of the war he experienced real mountains for the first time, tagging along on a works outing his sister had organised from her aircraft factory to Aberglaslyn in Snowdonia. When he saw the sublime mass of the

---

2-18 Lansdowne Lane, London, long back, 1967

The ragged backs of houses in Charlton, south-east London, with their irregular rooflines and a hotchpotch of wash-houses, sheds and yards cluttered with boxes, tin baths and broken fences. This drawing was sketched on site in 1967 before the houses were demolished to build a block of flats. It was later worked up into a series of vignettes representing the houses comprehensively (reproduced on page 90).

Pencil on paper, 13 x 36 cm. FHA 03/19

Falcon's bedsit in Putney, 1967

This drawing shows the Victorian house in which Falcon Hildred was living in London in the late 1960s. He occupied an attic bed-sitting room at the front and had a work room at the back dedicated to his drawing board. The furnishings were simple and modern. The drawing was done for his mother after she had visited.

Sepia pen and wash, 30 x 21 cm. FHA 06/07

Housing clearance at New Cross, 1977

This drawing reflected Falcon's feeling, developed over many years, that whole areas of seemingly good housing in London and elsewhere was being needlessly destroyed for redevelopment. The emptiness of the abandoned streets, the blank fencing in front of the cleared site and the blocked up windows of the terrace beyond capture his sense of desolation.

Pencil and watercolour on paper, 14 x 23 cm. FHA 03/61

---

mountains, the rocks and streams, and the walls and cottages that fought to tame this tough environment, he knew immediately he had found something that was going to be important to him. While living in London he had loved visits to the Yorkshire Dales and other uplands, but eventually it was Snowdonia that worked its magic on him. The town of Blaenau Ffestiniog became the centre of his fascination – the place known as 'the hole in the National Park' because the Snowdonia National Park boundary was drawn to exclude its prodigious man-made landscape. Falcon was enthralled to find a working-class industrial town in a mountain setting and to explore the intricate systems of quarries, workshops, tramways, settlements and reservoirs that had given the town its living. He and Rita came back again and again to camp in this remarkable setting. Blaenau became one of his most important subjects, and it was here he found a place to settle.

Since 1969, when he bought the former Pant-yr-ynn mill in Blaenau Ffestiniog, Falcon has established a remarkable model for living, focused around his life's work of cherishing industrial heritage. He turned the mill into a unique home, workplace and museum. In its consistency, integrity and purposefulness it recalls some famous homes connected with art or artists, such as the sculptor Barbara Hepworth's studio in St Ives, the live-in gallery of art historian and curator Jim Ede at Kettle's Yard in Cambridge, or Charleston, the Bloomsbury Group house in East Sussex.

Falcon has welcomed visitors to his mill and gallery for some forty years, yet arriving at Melin Pant-yr-ynn is like entering a secret world. The granite mill with its long slate roof and waterwheel sits under a crag above the settlement of Bethania, on the road south out of Blaenau Ffestiniog. The entrance lies above a high wall of boulders that makes a shelf on the steep hillside. The site is hidden from the lane below it, yet when you turn onto the terraced approach a panoramic view opens out across Bethania and Blaenau to the ridge line of the Moelwyns beyond. Manod mountain sweeps down to the back wall of the mill, and on his acre or so of land Falcon has nurtured the mountain's natural environment of waterfall, rock, birch and heather. You enter the mill's blank gable end through a plain, plank doorway painted oxide red that offers no hint of what lies beyond. Inside, you find a slab floor and whitewashed walls with glazed partitions that separate Falcon's drawing office from a workshop, a comfortable viewing room and stairs to his living accommodation above. Beyond this lies the great space of the mill, open to the roof. There is a smell of oil and grease, coal and wood smoke. Your eye travels along the line-shafting to a glimpse of the working waterwheel that beats beyond the gable, the boarded panels that display pictures and an enormous collection of chimney pots, ironwork, gates, signs and other artefacts rescued by Falcon from buildings being demolished.

The mill was built sometime before 1845, when it was described in a lease as a slab mill, though the timber floor in the main part of the building suggests it may have originally been a woollen mill. It sawed and planed slate slabs brought down a track from Diffwys quarry for over twenty years until three steam-powered mills were built at the quarry itself. It languished for a short time, then was transformed into a school for seven years in the 1870s while a purpose-built school was being constructed. After this, it was converted (or reconverted) into a woollen mill, which it was to be for the longest part of its working life. Weaving machinery was installed in 1881 by Jacob Jones and Son and the mill was extended with additional bays at the north end. It worked in tandem with Moelwyn mill in Tan-y-grisiau until 1964, when both closed.[4] The machinery was scrapped, apart from some remaining line-shafting and the 24-feet diameter overshot waterwheel.

When Falcon found it in 1968 the mill was derelict and being sold as a potential site for a new bungalow. It was one of many large, disused buildings available at a price affordable for an artist in Blaenau Ffestiniog (coincidentally it was also at this time that the

Melin Pant-yr-ynn, Bethania, Blaenau Ffestiniog

The former slate slab mill and woollen mill has been Falcon Hildred's home since 1969. The mill at the far end is preserved for display and his accommodation is in the nearer late nineteenth-century extension. The overshot waterwheel was restored and remains in working order.

Photographs: Iain Wright, Royal Commission, 2011
DS2011_342_003 and DS2011_342_011, NPRN 28620

---

sculptor David Nash acquired Rhiw chapel as a home and studio at the other end of the town). Sadly, most such buildings decayed beyond use, and this could easily have been the fate of Melin Pant-yr-ynn: when Falcon bought it the mill's floorboards were rotten, the waterwheel was out of use, the roof was leaking. But Falcon was seeking a simple life, not luxury. He had been impressed by the journal of the American writer Henry David Thoreau (1817-1862) in

Details from Melin Pant-yr-ynn

Wood shavings made in the course of work, a window grille made from scrap iron, a collection of tools.
(All courtesy of Clive Hicks-Jenkins, 2012)

Enamel jugs and a glass sign.
(Both courtesy of Sally Wakelin, 2012).

the 1840s, which described his life in a shed at Walden Pond in Massachusetts, far from the clutter of civilisation. Falcon moved into the mill in October 1969 and for five years occupied his own shed, inside the building, constructed against a window. He used a little stove for cooking; he took his water from the mill-stream; he fought with the waterfall that hammered at the back door and flooded the front yard knee-deep so that he could not get in or out by either entrance.

Falcon was now self-employed and eking out what money he had to begin work on the restoration. With the help of his partner Carole he repaired the roof and the waterwheel first, then decided to convert just one end of the mill to live in. He developed an ethos, a philosophy, for the restoration and for living that he called his 'mill phil.' (more usually spelled 'milfil'). He wanted to make changes with the greatest respect to the building and its history, and he planned to earn a living only from work that he could describe as honourable. He left most of the mill relatively untouched, and he delights in the authentic griminess that it still retains. Even in his living accommodation, his philosophy has been that there should be nothing superfluous, everything beautiful. In using local materials and minimising his energy consumption he was far ahead of the sustainability movement. He still has no refrigerator or freezer, instead using the cold stone of the mill and an enamel water pail to keep things cool; he has no television, he keeps only a few books of his own. He made all the timber doors and much of the furniture and fittings, according to his own, simple designs, and found cheap

Interior of living room, Melin Pant-yr-ynn

The simplicity of Falcon's living accommodation in the mill demonstrates his commitment to not surrounding himself with art but making art of his surroundings with well-designed, functional tools and furniture. The focal point is on the 'signal box' window he installed and its view to the Moelwyns.

Photograph: Iain Wright, Royal Commission, 2011.
DS2011_342_034 - NPRN 28620

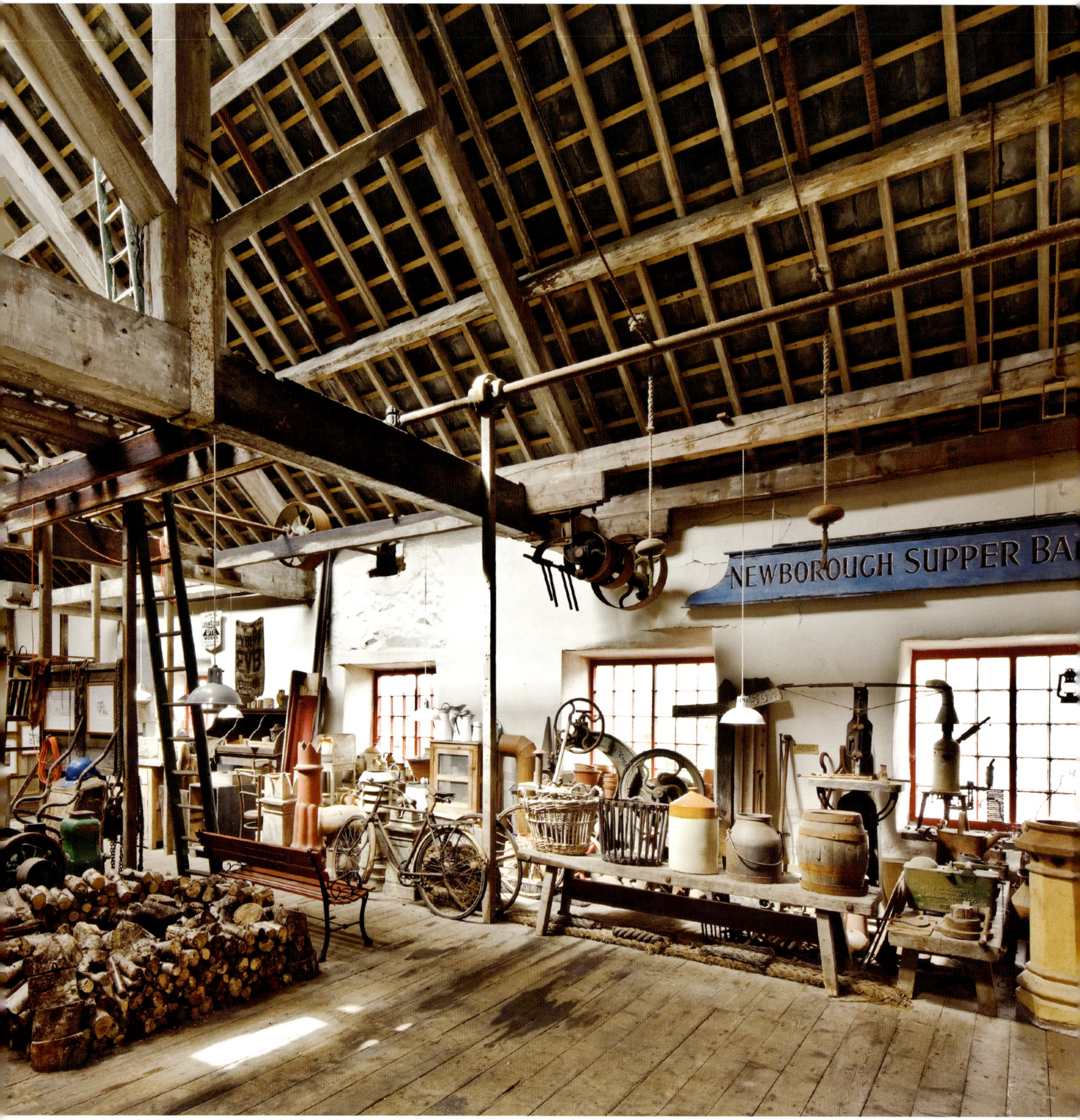
NEWBOROUGH SUPPER BA

Melin Pant-yr-ynn

These two views show the interior of the mill area, where Falcon has left the space open for visitors to see the mill, his displays, and artefacts collected over the years from buildings being demolished. Line shafting for the former woollen mill still runs through the roof trusses.

Photographs: Iain Wright, Royal Commission, 2011
DS2011_342_019 and DS2011_342_026 - NPRN 28620

and serviceable light switches and kitchen equipment. He reflects that his living accommodation has been functionally 'equipped' rather than 'furnished'. There are no artworks hanging on his walls because he ensures his household tools and utensils are functional objects of beauty – he has not surrounded himself with art but has made art of his surroundings.

'Milfil' has not just been an aesthetic experiment but a 'design for living' to give Falcon freedom and independence with which to do the work he considered important. He said in an interview in 2011,

> I can display what I like, I can work when I like, I can say what I like, and no one can sack me. And that freedom is one of the most valuable things in my life – how I spend my time, how I spend my money, what I choose to work on. It gives me the total freedom to fulfil my principles. I've made reality of my dreams and I can stick to my principles and I don't owe allegiance to anyone. That freedom is immensely valuable.

Falcon's adopted town has absorbed him as much as the mill he has restored. Having watched so many buildings be cleared away near his homes in Grimsby, Coventry and London, Falcon invested his energies not only in recording what was under threat but trying to find ways to fight the destruction. For him, Blaenau Ffestiniog is an unspoilt nineteenth-century working-class town:

> Whichever way you arrive the first thing you come to is a genuine stone house or a slate quarry. There isn't that fat ring of modern mediocrity which surrounds so many old towns nowadays. It still has its chapels – well some of them anyway – its workers' terrace houses, a railway viaduct, a pandy (fulling mill) and the remains of over twenty quarries. Also it is a stronghold of the Welsh language. So culturally and materially it is unusually complete. But it is a fragile completeness that needs care. Blaenau and its landscape are to slate what the Rhondda was to coal and Merthyr Tydfil to iron. It is as important now, historically, as a medieval walled town and needs to be respected as such.[5]

As a designer, Falcon has regarded practical conservation as being as much part of his work as recording. From as early as 1974 he campaigned to save buildings. In Blaenau he calls his study 'a record and vision' and he has tried to raise awareness and appreciation of the town's qualities and show how conservation can contribute to its future. This has taken the form of producing leaflets about the town, promotional posters, newspaper articles, exhibitions and designs. He has helped to save several buildings from demolition, including his own mill, Moelwyn mill and the houses at Uwchllaw'r Ffynnon. A particular focus has been on trying to create interest in the old market hall, even designing schemes for reuse and the restoration of an attractive public space around it. In the late 1990s the Snowdonia Society, with funding from Cadw and subscribers from

Poster '82-Blaenau Ffestiniog, 1982

Falcon has sought to raise awareness of what he sees as the exceptional qualities of Blaenau as a nearly complete Victorian working-class town. This bold design was produced as a poster in 1982 to mark the return to Blaenau of the restored Ffestiniog railway and the opening to the public of Pant-yr-ynn mill. At a time when threats to the townscape's integrity seemed at their greatest, the poster highlighted some of the town's qualities.

Copy of original ink design, 30 x 21 cm. FHA 01/158/01

Blaenau and elsewhere, commissioned him to document features in the townscape.

Recording Blaenau Ffestiniog and its surroundings has become a principal focus of Falcon's work in the last forty years. He has drawn the town, houses and chapels, the railways and inclines, and the dense, complex landscapes of the quarries and mines. Many of his subjects have disappeared in the time that he has been recording them, threatened by development in the same way as those

Market hall and square: drawing showing the interior of the market hall, 1994

Falcon's scheme for converting Blaenau Ffestiniog market hall into a heritage centre, adaptively reusing a redundant Victorian building. Although the scheme was not carried out, it helped to save the market hall from demolition.

Ink and watercolour on paper, 23 x 40 cm. FHA 01/178 - NPRN 41065

elsewhere but also here by the unstoppable forces of natural decay. Most buildings at the quarries have not been maintained for more than a generation, and many have been destabilised by the extreme microclimate – Blaenau is one of the wettest spots in Britain and the quarry workings rise to altitudes at risk of hard winter frosts. Recently, his own work has been complemented by surveys by the Royal Commission at representative slate industry sites and by research by other individuals, but for much of the last forty years if Falcon had not captured disappearing heritage no record of it would now exist.

He spent short periods away from Blaenau in the mid 1970s, teaching in Newcastle-upon-Tyne. Here, too, he made drawings of vanishing elements of townscape and industrial culture. This led him to think beyond the particular of the sites he was examining to seek a more general statement about the nature of nineteenth-century industrial culture. He drew this together under the title 'Worktown', and the whole became in his own mind a lifelong project. The first exhibition using the Worktown name came about in 1976, bringing together images from Grimsby, Coventry, Blaenau and elsewhere. It remains an eloquent title to describe his interests and achievement. With the concept now clear in his mind, Falcon embarked in the 1980s on two extensive projects focused on urban landscapes in south Wales.

First, Falcon was offered an exhibition at the Andrew Knight Gallery, a commercial art gallery in Cardiff run by the former director of visual arts at the Arts Council of Wales. Exceptionally for Falcon, this was arranged as a selling exhibition. Consequently, most of the works produced were dispersed into private collections,

Blaenau Ffestiniog town centre designs A and B, 2009, 2010

Falcon's two design schemes for improving Blaenau Ffestiniog town centre and saving the market hall and other threatened historic buildings. Scheme A has been adopted and a version of it is being built. Falcon's aim was to consolidate the town's distinctiveness, to create a place that would be of high-quality design yet still feel homely.

Ink and wash on paper, each 29 x 42 cm.
Top: FHA 01/199, above: FHA 01/200

Roof repairs, 1978

Sketched on site in June 1978, this little drawing captures the small scale of Blaenau's streets compared with the slate tips that loom over them.

Pencil and watercolour on paper,
26.5 x 14 cm
FHA 01/057 - NPRN 305760

Hen Gwaith Sets, Manod granite quarry, 1984

Manod or Madoc quarry still produced dolerite setts for making road surfaces only a few hundred metres from Falcon's home in Blaenau Ffestioniog, when he arrived there. It operated from the late nineteenth century until around 1972. Falcon refers to it by its Welsh name, 'Hen Gwaith Sets' – the Old Setts Works. By 1984 the buildings were decaying rapidly under the tough Snowdonia winters – deterioration emphasised by a conjuring of weather conditions rare for the artist.

Pencil and watercolour on paper, 21 x 30 cm.
FHA 01/059 - NPRN 415616

leaving the artist with only his preparatory drawings and sketches. Since that exhibition, Falcon has tended to sell only prints, preferring to see the originals kept together as a cumulative archive. Cardiff provided some excellent subjects. The whereabouts of many of the drawings are not currently known but Falcon has retained colour slides of them that have been scanned for the National Monuments Record of Wales.[6]

In 1987, Falcon was commissioned by Newport Museum and Art Gallery's Keeper of Art, Roger Cucksey, to record aspects of the townscape in celebration of the museum's centenary the following year, supported by funding from the Victoria and Albert Museum. Nearly all of the drawings went directly into the collection at Newport, and they constitute a vivid account of the town at this point in its history, of houses, public buildings, parks, streetscapes, chapels, docks. The drawings were exhibited at the museum under the title 'Newport Now'. Rightly prominent among the drawings were those of the towering Newport Transporter Bridge, which carried vehicles over the River Usk on a gondola suspended from a beam high enough for ships to pass beneath.

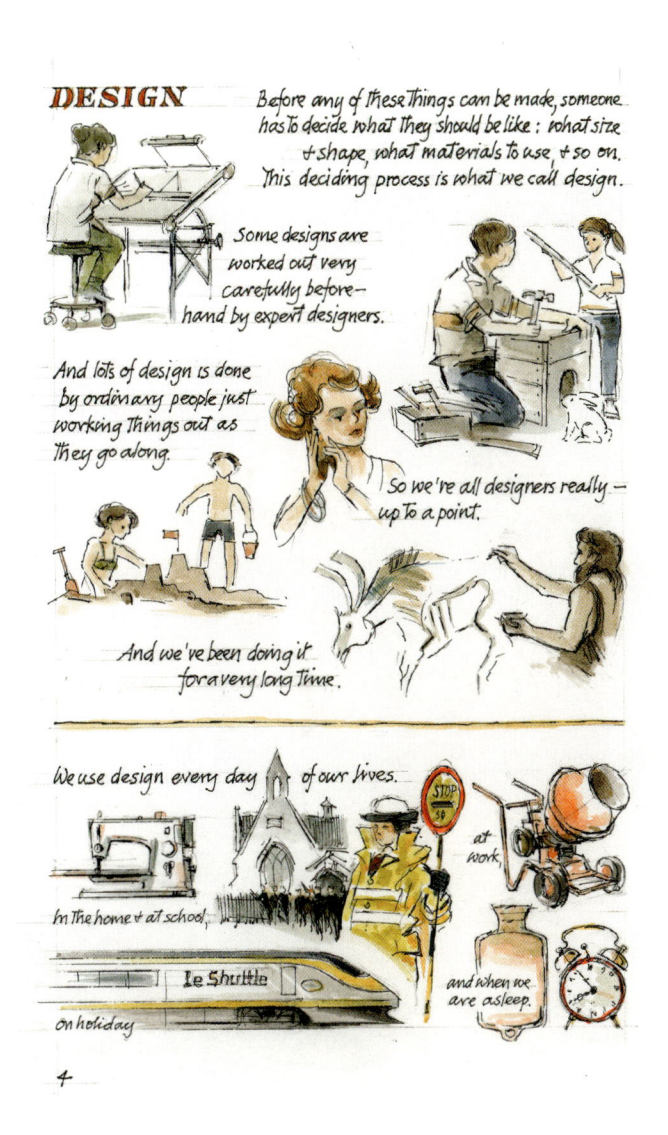

Travelling to and from Newport and Cardiff gave Falcon opportunities to see parts of the Valleys as he passed through, such as Merthyr Tydfil and Abercynon, and to produce sporadic sketches. He was so impressed with Newport Transporter Bridge that he went back to undertake more detailed work. This monumental structure was under threat of demolition at the time, having been out of use since 1985. However, a major programme of refurbishment was

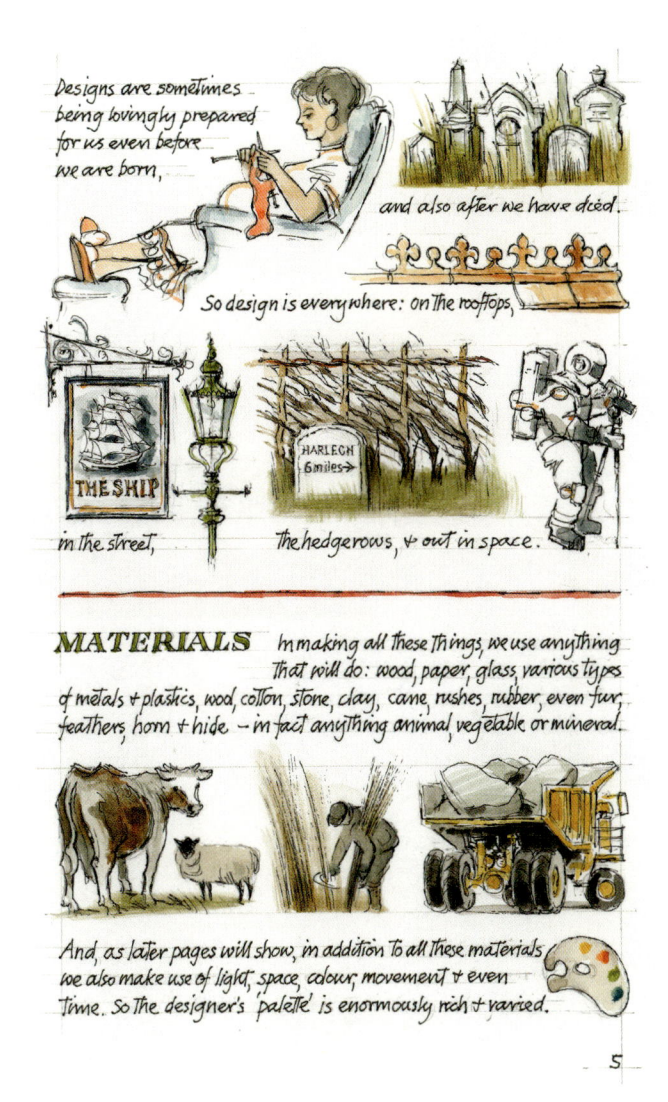

Original page layouts for A Word in Your Eye: or What is Design, 2001

Designed, illustrated, written and hand-lettered by Falcon Hildred, this introduction to design was published in 2001 by the National Centre for Product Design and Development at the University of Wales Institute, Cardiff. This double-page spread sets out initial concepts of design and materials and shows Falcon's holistic approach to what design is and what it is for.

Ink and watercolour on paper, 42 x 30 cm. FHA 07/07/03

begun that was eventually to result in it reopening to traffic in 1995. To celebrate the restoration Falcon wrote a book illustrated with over eighty drawings, published by Newport Museum and Art Gallery.[7] It was striking how his images showed the bridge in enormous detail yet made the mechanism readily understood – though understanding the mechanism is challenging for most people even while watching the real thing at work. He has described his approach:

The best way to understand anything mechanical is to take it apart and see if you can put it all back together again properly. This, in a way, is how I set about drawing the bridge. I took it apart and laid all the pieces out in a series of five drawings, one showing the workshop, and all the various things in there; another showing what you would see as you went onto the gondola, and so on. In this way I broke it all down into manageable sized chunks. [...] Yet even when I understood it all myself, I still had to find a way of explaining everything without rambling on or becoming too technical. So, to keep myself in check I imagined I was giving a guided tour of the bridge, and in my party were some engineers who knew all about bridges and so would quickly spot if I made a mistake. With them were their partners who knew nothing about engineering but were willing to learn, provided I kept it simple and interesting. Then I imagined I had some school children who were probably working on a special project such as tides or electric traction. [...] Then, as every experienced guide has learned, I had to anticipate the unexpected questions, such as 'which way is the sea?' or 'what were the tickets like?' Finding some of the answers sometimes meant making a special journey all the way from north Wales, or climbing all the way up onto the boom.[8]

In recognition of his contribution to the appreciation of the structure Falcon was invited to become a Vice-President of the Friends of Newport Transporter Bridge. He remarked that for someone whose drawings so often served to record something about to be destroyed, it was a joy to celebrate a reopening instead.

Over the last thirty years Falcon has added to his personal recording some highly visible commissions for sites that were not under threat. For Cadw he designed lithographs for a series marking its creation as a body in 1986, making atmospheric drawings of Caerphilly Castle and Llanthony Priory. For Gwynedd Council he has made illustrations and explanatory text interpreting the buildings and machinery of the estate workshops at Parc Glynllifon near Caernarfon, including the sawmill and gasworks. For a friend he produced a set of drawings recording the elegant Georgian

An aerial photograph of Fort Belan taken by the Royal Commission in 1998 provides an interesting comparison with Falcon's image.
DI2005_0688 - NPRN 26459

fortifications of Fort Belan on the Menai Strait in 1997. Comparison with a Royal Commission aerial photograph of the site shows how powerfully Falcon's drawings complement other methods of documentation, providing an informative and unambiguous form of interpretation.

A significant departure from documenting buildings was a book commissioned by the University of Wales Institute, Cardiff, to introduce young people to design and the ideas behind it. Falcon not only wrote and illustrated the book, *A Word in your Eye: or What is Design?*, but hand-lettered the whole text. The book beautifully and convincingly explains his philosophy of design in a readily accessible way and would be a good introduction for anyone to the host of ways in which designers and the designed interact with everyday life. At around the same time Falcon won recognition for his lifetime's achievement in recording buildings by being made an Honorary Member of the Royal Society of Architects in Wales.

What does Falcon hope to achieve by his recording? Simply producing a record that will outlast the building or monument itself is an outcome of great importance to him. He estimates that about nine-tenths of the buildings he has recorded have since been demolished or changed beyond recognition. For this reason he feels compelled to seek more than skin-deep appearance to provide documentation of a form that will allow a building to be understood by future generations not privileged to see the real thing:

> *I'm taking something that may well come down, be demolished, and I'm putting it back on paper. I'm doing it as authentically as I can. I don't use artist's licence. I draw what's there, or I may draw x-ray views, or cutaways, or bird-eye views to explain what's there. I draw what I understand rather than simply what's in front of me.*

Fort Belan, 1997

The first of two compendium views of Fort Belan, a polygonal militia fort begun in 1775 and a dock of the 1820s that guarded the western entrance to the Menai Strait. Falcon added captions to explain the operation of the site and its architectural and defensive features.

Ink and watercolour on paper, 46 x 57 cm.
FHA 02/67/01 - NPRN 26459

In rare cases another outcome has been that bringing positive attention to a building has resulted in its protection, and indeed Falcon has campaigned for buildings to be listed. However, the availability of a permanent record remains valuable even where buildings survive. Buildings that are listed may still be at risk of demolition or natural decay, while those that find new uses may be

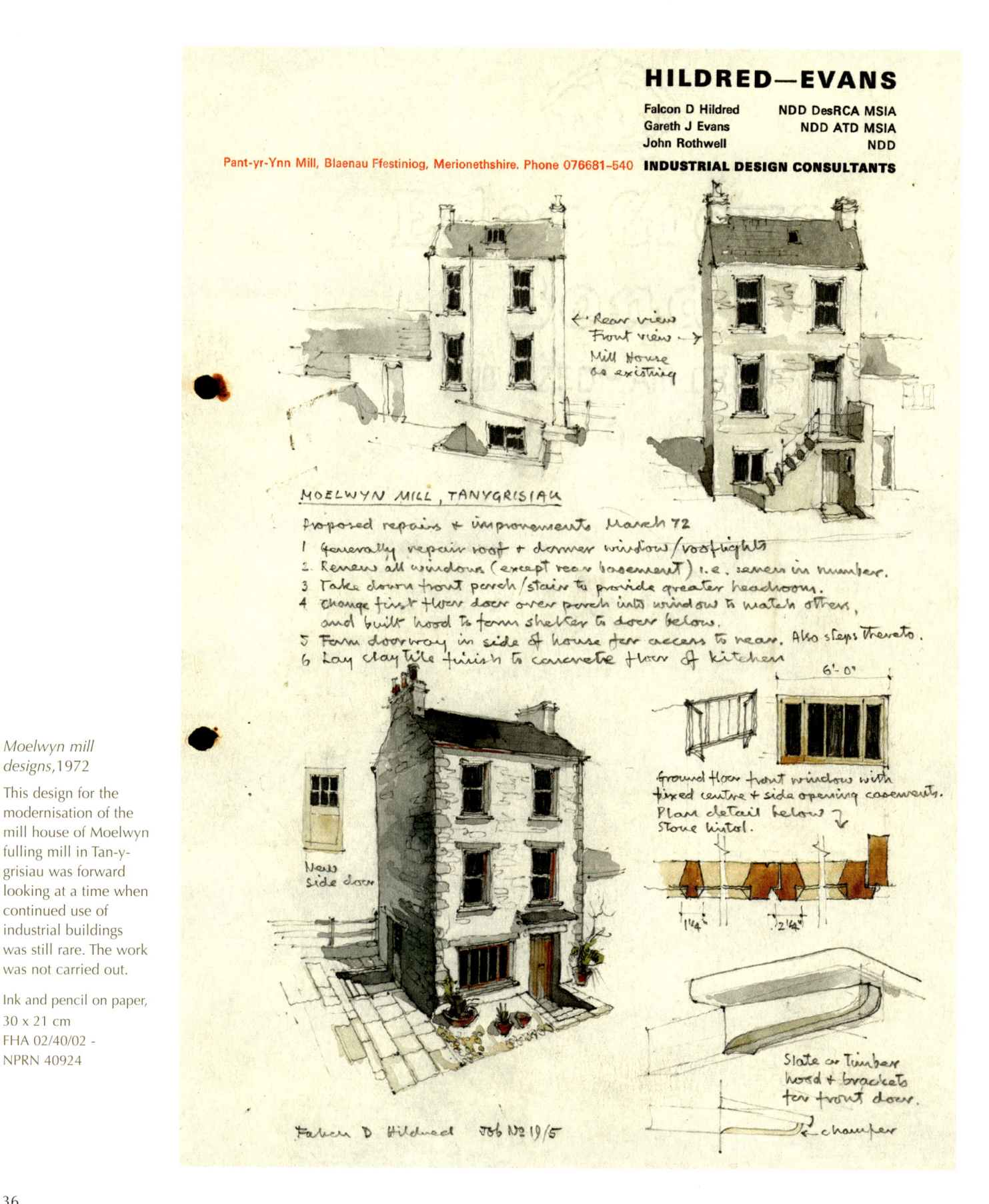

Moelwyn mill designs, 1972

This design for the modernisation of the mill house of Moelwyn fulling mill in Tan-y-grisiau was forward looking at a time when continued use of industrial buildings was still rare. The work was not carried out.

Ink and pencil on paper, 30 x 21 cm
FHA 02/40/02 - NPRN 40924

preserved in a different form from that which Falcon was able to observe. A telling example for him was a row of run down and disused cottages in Blaenau Ffestiniog that were listed and in due course restored. During this process he watched how new materials, new boundaries and new lifestyles within, while they saved the buildings for the future, changed their nature. Even sites conserved for the purposes of heritage have been compromised in his eyes through being tidied up and added to with picnic areas, shops, trees, signs and banners, and he notes ruefully that he wouldn't draw them now. In other cases, though, design work of real quality has achieved a happy balance of new uses with old patina and personality. Falcon has himself been involved in design work occasionally, bringing to bear some of his own 'milfil'.

Whether a subject survives or not, another benefit that Falcon hopes his drawing will achieve is the celebration and promotion of craftsmanship and character. The thrill in a subject for Falcon often derives from his sense of the quality and attentiveness with which buildings and artefacts were created. Appreciation of the craftsmanship and pride of people in the ages before modern materials and mass production has been one of the driving forces of his work. In fact, buildings are just one expression of it. Asked about his influences, he cites not artists or illustrators, or even architecture, but the folk art created by ordinary working people who made the things they used. A seminal experience for him as a young man was attending the agricultural show at Stoneleigh in Warwickshire:

> I went around a corner and there in front of me was this magnificent sight, so beautiful I was almost in tears. It was a horse-drawn brewer's dray. Everything about it was perfect, right down from the men high up on their seat with their bowler hats, moustaches and spotless shirts, waistcoats and aprons. They really looked the part. Then the horses, truly magnificent and beautiful of course, with their polished harness work, every stitch and buckle superbly crafted, as was every bolt and chamfer, piece of metalwork and lettering on the dray, right down to how the barrels had been placed. All of it was faultlessly handsome, yet perfectly functional too. No effort had been spared to get everything right, yet there was nothing superfluous either. I was looking at the art of good design. And that's how we should build and make things: with care, skill, imagination, beauty, intelligence and respect.[9]

The nature of Falcon's recording varies from highly rendered depictions to swift site sketches, intended to show an isolated detail or the broad shape of a building and how it sits in its landscape. The sketches are often full of detail and are complete in their own right, if time and weather conditions permitted him to work on. Sometimes, however, they are the briefest of notes, capturing an idea or a recollection. A tiny sketch of Abercynon Miners' Institute, for example, done on a torn scrap of paper in just a minute or two

Abercynon miners' institute, 1987 (detail)

A swift sketch of the enormous miners' institute at Abercyon near Pontypridd captures its cheek-by-jowl relationship to the surrounding houses and proud stance on the sloping site.

Felt pen and watercolour on paper, 9.5 x 7.5 cm.
FHA02/75 - NPRN 85865

while passing by in 1987, captures the enormous ambition of this great voluntary enterprise, the building rising on the other side of the valley like an ocean liner cutting through the waves of terraced houses. In just a few swift strokes the sketch conjures the building's colourful detailing. Sadly, Falcon was unable to go back to study it more closely and a few years later this miners' institute, like so many others, was gone forever.

An important group of Falcon's most highly finished drawings show memories of places or reconstructions of how they may once have looked. The fullest of these are rich with mood. Many are night-time or dusk views projecting a stark and gloomy vision of past industrial life, sometimes evoking the distinctive nocturnes of the Yorkshire-born Victorian artist John Atkinson Grimshaw (1836-1893). One of the most successful is the reconstruction of Eli Green's 'cottage factory' in Coventry, seen as though in the silk-weaving depression of 1860. Falcon knew the buildings intimately, having recorded them with numerous site drawings while they were derelict and due for demolition (see page 156-161). The factory design was a response to the domestic nature of silk ribbon weaving in Coventry in the mid-nineteenth century. Weavers wanted to remain their own masters, but as a step towards mechanisation and economies of

Eli Green's cottage factory, Coventry, 1969

One of the artist's most emotive views. The darkness, empty streets and rain evoke visually the depression of Eli Green's factory in 1860, when new tariffs put thousands of silk weavers out of work. The view is from Barry Street in Hillfields, looking towards the steam engine house in the middle of the triangle of three-storey houses with powered workshops on their top floors. The buildings were completely cleared in the post-war clearances. Even the name Eli Green's Triangle, by which the block had always been known, disappeared after the apex of the triangular site was removed in a road-widening scheme.

Chalk and ink on paper, 16 x 38 cm. FHA 03/84/02

scale Eli Green, in 1858-9, built rows of three-storey weavers' houses to form a triangle with a steam engine at its centre. There were sixty-seven cottages with kitchens and parlours on the ground floor, bedrooms on the first floor and workshops on top, following the traditional layout of ribbon weavers' houses. The 'topshop' floor's large windows and height above the street allowed good light for the painstaking work, but the innovation in premises of this period was that the looms were provided with power through drive shafts at roof level from a steam engine. The weavers worked from home but paid rent for the houses and fees if they wanted to attach belt drives to their looms and use the power supplied. But disaster followed in 1860, just a year after the factory was completed, when the Cobden Treaty removed import tariffs on French and Swiss ribbons. Within a few months, thousands of Coventry ribbon weavers were out of work and seeking to emigrate. Falcon says:

What's important to record? Do you record the factory or do you record the helpless depression of it once it had been built? Well, I decided to record both. I made measured drawings, very careful drawings. It's all there. But in five of the drawings I've gone solely for mood, for the atmosphere. [...] It's like recording the unrecordable, and it was a very, very important aspect of my choice of subject.

Other reconstructions relate to houses in London that had gone by the time Falcon could take an interest, so he sought to bring communities back to life from Ordnance Survey maps, photographs, surviving clues and the recollections of local people. Some drawings have been based on his own early memories, for example of seeing an unemployed man playing the trumpet for money in Depression-era Grimsby (page 14) or watching labourers and their horse-drawn wagons returning to the corporation workshops in Coventry in 1941, presumably after a day clearing bomb damage.

Then there are the explanatory images. Some of these are solely

Lyford Street, Woolwich

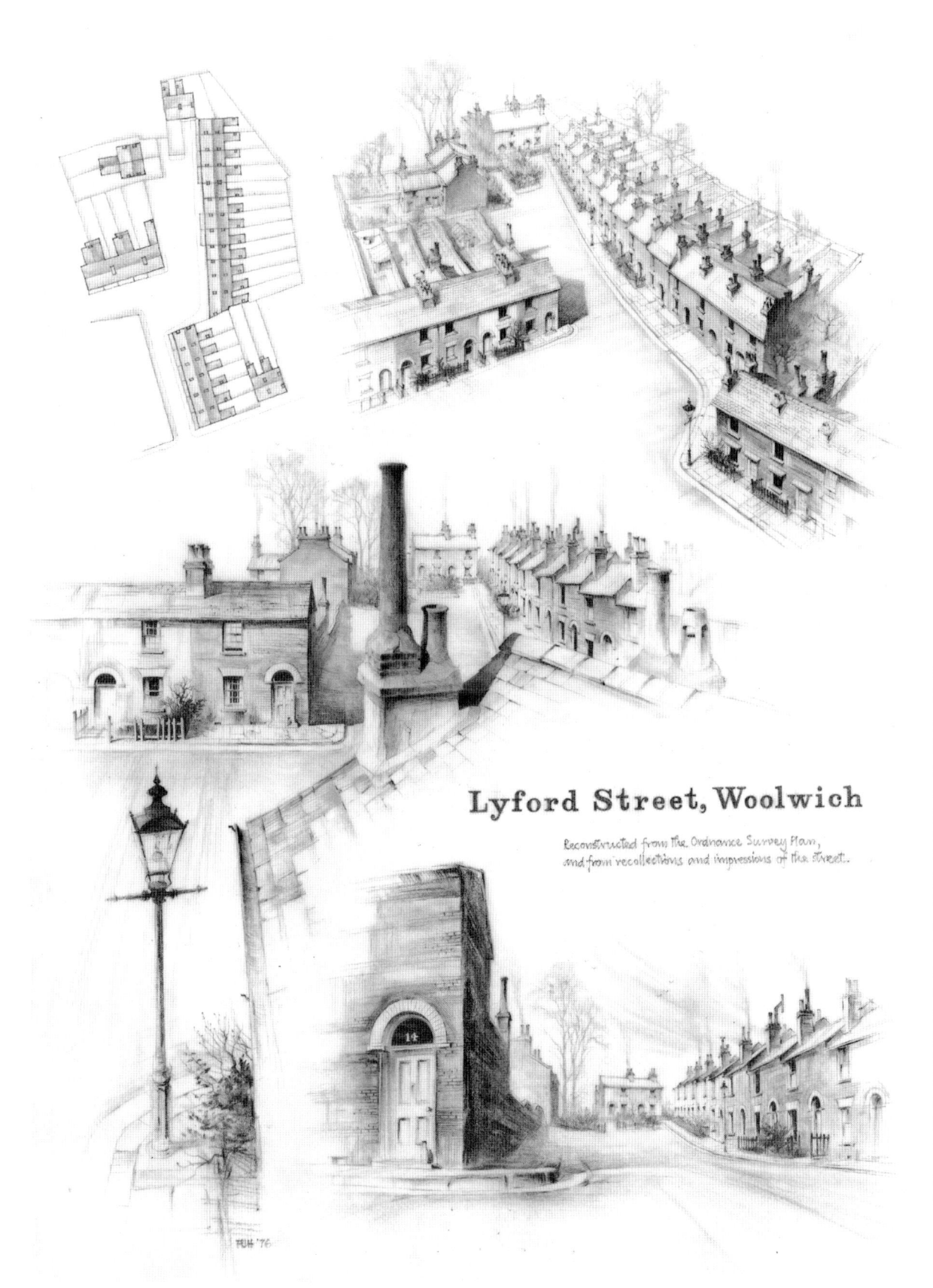

Reconstructed from the Ordnance Survey Plan, and from recollections and impressions of the street.

Lyford Street, Woolwich, 1976

Falcon's reconstruction from documentary sources and site notes made prior to demolition of a close of Victorian terraced houses near Woolwich Dockyard in London SE18. The houses were demolished in the early 1960s but the expected redevelopment did not come for some thirty years. The drawing gives a rounded impression of the former buildings, with a plan aerial perspective and two ground views in one image.

Pencil on paper, 32 x 22 cm.
FHA 03/16

Returning home, Coventry corporation stables, 1979

The drawing was based on observations in 1941, when Falcon had only just arrived in Coventry as a boy. It shows labourers and wagons returning to the depot, probably after clearing the remains of the Coventry Blitz the year before.

Pencil and watercolour on paper, 10 x 10 cm. FHA 03/50

Cash's chimney, 1976

A detailed elevation drawing of the chimney for the steam engine boilers at the weaving factory of J. J. Cash, Coventry, built in 1857. The whole height of the chimney is shown, from lightning conductor to plinth, to scale, with every brick course suggested. Unlike an architectural elevation, however, the drawing shows the chimney not as new but as it appeared more than a century later, with the patterns of weathering and no doubt alterations of detail.

Gelatine print with watercolour, 84 x 14 cm. FHA 03/03/02

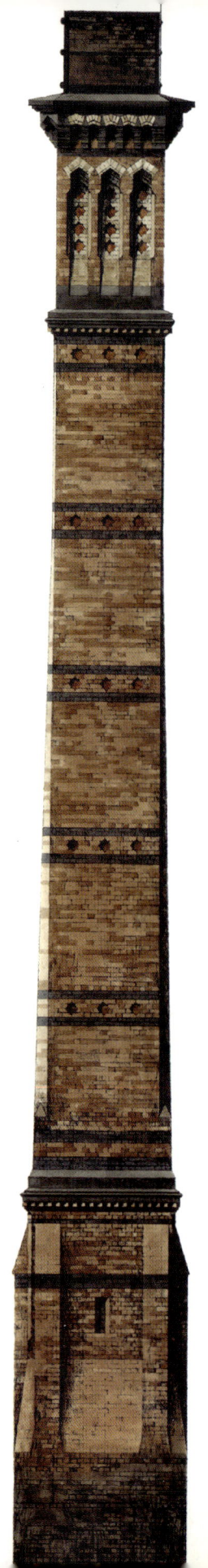

Old Glamorgan library and registry, Cardiff, preliminary drawing, 1987

Falcon's sensibility about how buildings function in urban space and contribute to quality of life is expressed succinctly in this drawing and accompanying note. The library and clerks' office was built in 1881 and later became the Glamorgan Staff Club. It was listed in 1999 and survives. It fills an unusual, three-sided site in central Cardiff, facing Westgate Street on the left, Quay Street, and Womanby Street on the right.

Line copy and watercolour on paper, 12 x 14.5 cm.
FHA 02/72 - NPRN 301223

---

architectural, and simply show a building as clearly as possible, in a way one could not possibly see it, even if it still existed. An example is Falcon's painting showing a single elevation of the enormous chimney of Cash's weaving factory in Coventry, done in 1976. This is a precise drawing. The correct number of brick courses has been calculated (though Falcon hastens to point out that the thousands of individual bricks are suggested rather than individually drawn). A real view of the chimney would see it either from a distance, cluttered and obscured by other buildings or, if close-up, in a perspective that dwindled to almost nothing at the top. Falcon found his appreciation of the chimney's design growing to admiration as he drew it so meticulously. It tapered elegantly as it rose and was simply decorated to break up the massive volume with bands of blue and star motifs made from bricks with their corners chamfered off. The original drawing went to the Victoria and Albert Museum in London but Falcon produced prints of it, some of which were hand-coloured. He remembers,

> When I was painting the prints, the last thing I did was put in the bands of blue brick that punctuate the height, and I was quite

Old Glamorgan library and registry, Cardiff, study of corner of building, 1987

A simple study, this drawing nevertheless captures the strong architectural effect created by the detailing of a façade with relief: a quality of Victorian buildings that tends to be forgotten in modern buildings or omitted as too costly.

Line copy and watercolour on paper, 20 x 12 cm.
FHA 02/71 - NPRN 301223

> startled to see just how much this simple touch added vitality to the design. This was particularly noticeable when compared to the prints which didn't have the bands. They give the structure a rhythm like the beat of a piece of music.[10]

It is the height of contradiction to be putting up Victorian-style lamp-posts & bollards, & then to pull down two genuine Victorian buildings.

Blaenau Ffestiniog Market Place with its hall, hotel, orderly row of shops, pub & chapel, all grouped round an intimate open space, forms an ideal centre for community life, & would be an excellent starting point for the town's regeneration.
All the buildings are relatively good architecturally, & the whole group is a perfect example of Victorian town planning — something which many towns have lost & are now spending millions on trying to re-create.

Above: Blaenau Market Square as it could be.
Below: What is proposed

Demolition is final & permanent. The landscaping that has been proposed, is only a quick-fix & an admission of failure to think of something better. In fact, in this case it's only a fancy word for carpark.
Do you ever visit a town or go on holiday somewhere to see their carparks? Carparks don't regenerate, they deaden.

Pavers & bollards are a passing fashion. They're appearing all over the country making everywhere look alike. Blaenau needs change, but it must keep its identity & character, not end up looking like everywhere else.

Those 19th century towns that modernised their old centres, are not better off now but worse, because not only have they lost their character & history, they now have serious social problems of vandalism & violence. A good environment is a civilising influence. Break up the Market Square & you begin to destroy Blaenau.

Yes, it *will* cost more to restore the Market Square. Much more. But it will give much better value too, & for far longer. Isn't that what regeneration is about? That's the big difference between us & the Victorians. Whereas they paid whatever it cost to do a job well, we're always looking for cost savings. And it shows. This is why we're going back to Victorian-style lamp-posts. You got what you pay for. Cost-saving has not worked. So it's no good thinking we can really solve problems & go into the 21st century & regeneration, with values, attitudes & policies that are way out of date, & have been proved to fail.
Many of the inner-city problems of today, are due not to decaying Victorian buildings, but to the failure of the 'Urban Renewal' of the 60's.
The utilitarian, cost-conscious, philistine mentality of this century has produced a bleak & shoddy environment, which people from Prince Charles downwards are sick of.

No two carvings are the same

Above: some of the details that make the buildings of the Market Square so attractive, & below: what they plan to replace it all with

Falcon intends some drawings as explanatory images to make particular points. This was the case throughout his book, *A Word in Your Eye*, but also in sketches intended to raise issues or pose questions, for example pointing out the delicate qualities of decoration in Victorian buildings or showing how a building functions in the townscape. His drawing of a Victorian ventilation grille is a fine example of his ability to explain the subtle accumulation of geometry that goes to make a workaday object rich in carefully considered pattern. Other images take this further, becoming themselves designs or envisionings, as in his proposal drawings for how Blaenau Ffestiniog could look if buildings were put to new uses rather than demolished to make way for additional car parking. This is something he cares deeply about, and making explanatory drawings has been his own way of initiating a campaign. 'I paint and draw because it's my language, it's the one in which I can be most eloquent.'

Thoughtful and accurate drawing is probably the oldest method of architectural or archaeological recording, yet it still possesses sensitivities that photography or more modern technologies do not. It complements other methods. In particular, as a technique that involves interpretation and synthesis rather than the unmediated capture of information, it is a powerful tool to aid understanding and appreciation.

One of the greatest differences between drawing and photography concerns the limitations of the lens. It is almost impossible to capture with a camera a subject that surrounds the viewer, such as machinery in the confined space of a cider mill interior (page 186). Of course laser scans create an accurate and objective simulacrum; but measured drawings or perspectives enable the contents of a building to be seen and understood as humans present would see and understand them. The limitations of the camera are apparent outside too. Drawings can encompass space whereas (as the painter David Hockney among others has argued) the one-eyed lens fails to capture distance or surroundings truthfully, seeing only in a narrow frame equivalent to tunnel vision, or else with a fish-eye that pushes the central subject far away. Falcon's panoramas encapsulate a whole scene in a way that seems close to human perception and they allow

---

Market hall and square, Blaenau Ffestiniog, illustrated letter, 1995

In this drawing Falcon sought to capture some of the qualities of Blaenau Ffestiniog as an urban environment and draw attention to the values that could be lost. He contrasted in particular the market hall square as it could be, with market stalls and people circulating, with the proposal to demolish the hall and turn the whole area into a car park. The market hall was saved but its future is still uncertain.

Colour photocopy, 42 x 30 cm. FHA 01/161/02 - NPRN 410658

Maenofferen quarry, second site study, 1999

This panoramic drawing, sketched at one of Blaenau Ffestiniog's slate mines when it was still working, takes in far more than a camera could do. Without the distortions of the lens, it parallels what a visitor experiences and lets the eye travel across the landscape. The entrance to the underground workings is beneath the viewpoint, with the inclined rail tracks dropping towards it from the winding house. Trucks passed in a tunnel through the bluff of rock behind the winding house to the slate mill on the right, and then down railed inclines to the valley beyond. Further drawings are on pages 180-81.

Pencil, ink and watercolour on paper, 23 x 66 cm.
FHA 01/012/02 - NPRN 400427

the eye to detour and hover, tracing the outline of a ridge or following the path of a tramway: an experience much more akin to being in the real space and seeing with 270-degree binocular perception. The consequences are not just accurate representation: Falcon's drawings have a capacity to rekindle some of the excitement of the real places that compares well with photography. He tries to draw not just the visible facts but his relationship with his subject and what he knows about it: at its best, he says, 'the eye and the hand and your feelings, your emotions, are all working.'

So much is relatively obvious. What is more surprising about Falcon's expert drawing is the way in which he can perceive and record details that the camera somehow misses. We think the camera never lies, but it can. This is why Falcon always makes a sketch on site, even when using his camera to provide an additional aide memoire. He gives an example of how he did a quick sketch in Cardiff one very cold winter day and took photographs too with the intention of working up a finished drawing when he got home. He realised the crudeness of his photograph in the process:

> One of the reasons I drew the building was that it had a slightly ornamental gable. But this wasn't at all clear in the photograph when I came to look at it later, which I thought was strange, because I don't invent things. So I checked with the site sketch and it was there clearly enough, but you would never have noticed it in the photograph. So what had happened? Well, without realising it, I'd used a touch of emphasis to bring out the character of the building and show what I thought was interesting about it. But this wasn't artist's licence. I wasn't telling a lie; quite the opposite. I was just using the slightest exaggeration to bring out the truth and make things clearer, intuitively making choices: that's what caught my eye, that's what interested me, and so that's what I wanted to show. So in drawing one isn't just replicating what's there, one is imbuing the work with feeling, understanding, character and human warmth. I suppose this is the artist's way and this is what gives art its appeal. The camera can't do this [...]. So in the end I just left the sketch as it was.[11]

The veracity Falcon describes has become more important to him as time has gone by. One can detect a gradual stylistic change from his densely worked and atmospheric studies of industrial settlements under darkening skies in the 1960s and 1970s to more factual drawings that record exactly what he sees. In this sense he has followed the opposite trajectory to many artists of long careers, who tend to become freer as they age, perhaps more moved to capture essentials of mood or form and less patient with detail – as for example in the cases of late Turner or late Monet. For Falcon, measurement and accuracy of scale and detail have become more valuable, not less.

Through the drive for exactitude, the Neo-Romanticism found in Falcon's earlier paintings has reduced over time, but up until the mid 1970s one can sense echoes of John Piper's atmospheric depictions of ruins, John Minton's illustrations or Alan Sorrell's moody period reconstructions of ancient sites and dense, dank gouaches of nature tearing at the seams of human constructions. These were artists of great impact in the mid-twentieth century, so it is hardly surprising if Falcon absorbed their influences, perhaps most clearly seen in his early and Piperesque Windmill, Coventry (page 188) or his Sorrell-like Blackdown mill, Warwickshire of 1966 (page 154). Indeed a Romantic philosophy still underlies Falcon's purposes – reflecting on his working process in this book he writes of buildings abandoned and reclaimed by nature that 'their silence seemed to crave a sympathetic listener'. Like him, many Neo-Romantic artists of the mid-twentieth century found particular inspiration in Wales, including Piper, David Jones, John Craxton, Graham Sutherland, and the Welsh-born Ceri Richards, Bert Isaac and John Elwyn.[12]

However, what has made Falcon's contribution unique is his passion to work with accuracy and authority: to make a permanent record that in a sense could fill the void that a building's disappearance might leave. He has an exceptional facility for pencil and watercolour technique that quickly and accurately captures his subject in the field. Compare his depictions of abandoned slate quarries with those of Isaac, who repeatedly drew the abandoned Dorothea quarry near Nantlle from the 1970s to the 1990s. Isaac's images are abstract, ambiguous, evocative of sensations, deeply coloured, and depict one site over and over again; Falcon's are minutely observed, sometimes incorporate measurements, offer complementary viewpoints, and seek to record as many subjects as possible. Falcon can in some regards be seen as a Realist, selecting not conventionally aesthetic subjects but the nitty-gritty of everyday surroundings, something that can be seen in other artists well known during his early career, such as the Camden Town realist Walter Richard Sickert (1860-1942) or the 'kitchen sink' painter John Bratby (1928-1992).

While just as emotive in their way as Isaac's expressive works, and just as honest as Bratby's domestic scenes, it is clear that Falcon's impressions are created in the mind of an archaeologist and designer: in many cases you could pick up a set of drawings and have all the information needed to reconstruct the building or make a model of it.

Some critics might say that this commitment to accurate recording makes Falcon's drawings not works of art at all but simply

John Piper (1903-1992), *Seaton Delaval, Northumberland,* about 1941

John Piper was the pre-eminent British painter of ruins and ancient monuments in the twentieth century. Although they shared interests in recording buildings, Piper's expressive use of colour and freedom of mark-making contrast with Falcon's approach to documentation. This painting is of the Vanbrugh mansion of Seaton Delaval in Northumberland. Piper felt the burned-out house echoed the wartime damage to British cities that he was recording at the same time.

Oil on canvas laid on board, 29 x 85 cm
Private collection. Copyright: The Piper Estate.

documents. If one judged the drawings individually and out of context, that might be a reasonable point. However, another way of seeing them is to identify Falcon's commitment as a whole artistic act. He works with the obsession of the true artist, not to make sales (most of his work never being made available for sale) or to fill galleries, but to satisfy his own need to create and depict. Such obsession and commitment to a personal way of seeing have often been marks of great artists: think of Van Gogh's determination to capture French peasant life or the obsession of the Cornish primitive artist Alfred Wallis with recapturing memories of his life at sea. One could also make comparisons with contemporary artists working in a conceptual idiom, such as Christo, whose artistic act has been to wrap up buildings all over the world as though they were giant parcels, or Richard Long, whose project has been to walk and to memorialise his walks in different ways. The output of both these artists has been their activities, and their documentation of them has been secondary. In the same way, Falcon's commitment has been not just to the products of his art but to an act of homage. Like them, he is an artist whose commitment adds up to much more than the sum of its parts and whose lifetime project has been a passion, a fervour.

One of the aims of this book and its associated exhibitions and web-based developments is to put right the wrong that Falcon's work is not well known. He is not widely recognised as a contemporary artist because his work is too individual, too purposeful, and because it sits outside current fashions. He is not seen as an archaeologist or historian because he generally records what he sees as an end in itself, rather than as a methodology with which to write histories or engage in academic debates.

For all this, though, people are strongly drawn to Falcon's work as visual art. His images are full of interest for many viewers who are fascinated by the skill, detail and often the humour with which he records things that are (or were) familiar to them. People who wander into his gallery at Melin Pant-yr-ynn or see his work at the Royal Commission frequently respond with engagement and excitement. For those wishing to document historic buildings and especially industrial sites and landscapes, his approach to drawing and his output as a whole may suggest some principles or lessons for their own approaches.

One group of lessons reinforces the value of drawing as a tool of recording alongside others. Falcon's work demonstrates that the properties and potential of the sketchbook still complement those of the camera or the laser scanner, for example enabling details to be understood and a sense of place to be captured, and challenging the recorder to look hard and examine the subject. The immediacy of perspective drawing, as opposed to technical plans and elevations, also has a value not found in other media in the way it engages people with its depictions – it not only 'draws out' a subject but 'draws in' an audience.

The second group of points that arise from Falcon's practice concerns the choices of what to record and when to record it. It is

Bert Isaac, *Quarry edge*, 1999

A painting by Bert Isaac of Dorothea quarry, Nantlle. Form, colour and the ambiguous depiction of the return of nature to abandoned places were Issac's interests, in contrast with Falcon's accurate accounts of buildings and industrial features.

Water-soluble media on paper, 73 x 57 cm
Contemporary Art Society for Wales, National Library of Wales.
Copyright: Joan Isaac.

clear from the fate of so much that he has documented over the years that the commonplace and typical, despite its apparent abundance, may be at least as threatened as the exceptional, and drawing those buildings and features that are generally taken for granted is likely to prove a valuable service as they are eroded by change – unaltered workers' terraced houses, timber windows, slate walls or industrial chimneys were all normal parts of the scenery when Falcon started recording them, but they are no longer. Falcon's approach also reinforces the point that the built environment is of value just as much for telling details, marks of use and textures, which are so easily lost, as for architectural style elements or major structures. But perhaps the most important lesson from Falcon's fifty-year projet is that it is always worth making a record while there is an opportunity, because tomorrow may be too late.

Finally, Falcon's effort in recent decades to keep all his drawings together and its recent accession into a national archive is a reminder that even the most valuable documentation is unlikely to be able to do its job if it has not been published or secured in a permanent archive where it will be consulted. Few artists, archaeologists or photographers give thought to how the results of their work will be shared.

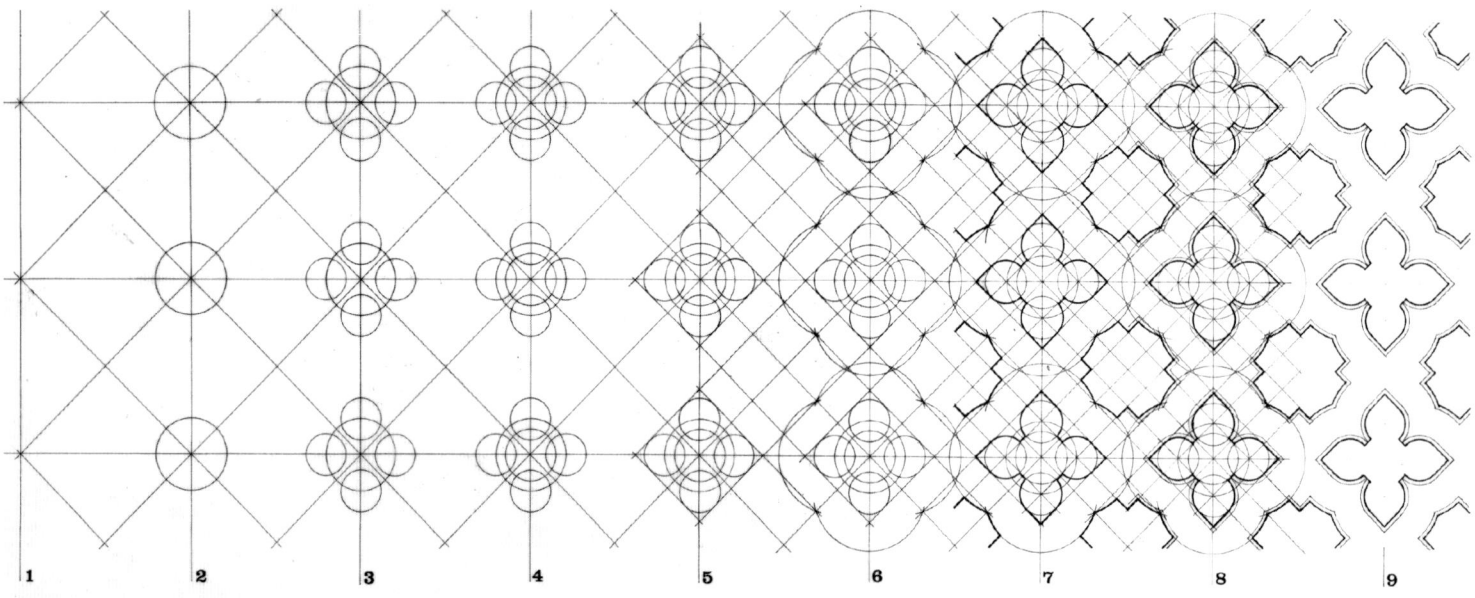

Geometry of an iron ventilation grille

For many years Falcon has retained his original work, believing that it should be kept together as a collection that could be used to widen appreciation and understanding of Britain's industrial culture. Almost all of this lifetime's work is now permanently preserved in the National Monuments Record of Wales in Aberystwyth, where it can continue to do what Falcon regards as 'its work'.

The safekeeping of the collection was made possible in 2011 by a partnership between the Royal Commission on the Ancient and Historical Monuments of Wales and Ironbridge Gorge Museum Trust, with a grant from the Heritage Lottery Fund and the support of the artist himself. As a result of this, a collection of well over 600 drawings is available for visitors to consult in person and is accessible in digital form for consultation online. This book ensures that the wealth of this material can be appreciated in context with other work by the artist at Ironbridge Gorge Museum and the extensive series commissioned by Newport Museum and Art Gallery.

The images reproduced here are a cross-section of about a third of these combined collections. They are already being put to use in a wide range of applications, and this can only grow as more people become aware of the wealth of the resource. Individual images are being used in research (for example in the Royal Commission's study of the Welsh slate industry), in education as resources for schools, in local studies, or just for enjoyment.

Above all, it is to be hoped that Falcon's drawings will inspire a deeper appreciation of our historic environment, in particular to keep alive an understanding of working-class industrial culture and a respect for what our forefathers achieved. The collection exists to allow the buildings that once stood for all of this to continue telling their stories to future generations.

Geometry of an iron ventilation grille, 1975

This sequence of geometrical construction lines shows the care and skill that went into designing an apparently simple and unimportant Victorian ventilation grille at a shop in Spon Street, Coventry.

Ink on tracing paper, 21 x 42 cm. FHA 03/74/01

Ynys Enlli, 2003

Ynys Enlli (Bardsey Island) is about two miles off the Llŷn peninsula in north Wales. The island is a Site of Special Scientific Interest and a National Nature Reserve, and is managed jointly by the Bardsey Island Trust, Cadw and the Countryside Council for Wales. This drawing is a study of the buildings on the island, showing a farmhouse and nearby housing. Bardsey Island lighthouse, built in the early 1820s, is also illustrated with the lighthouse keeper's house in the foreground.

Pencil, ink and watercolour on paper, 31 x 42 cm. FHA 02/24 - NPRN 402783

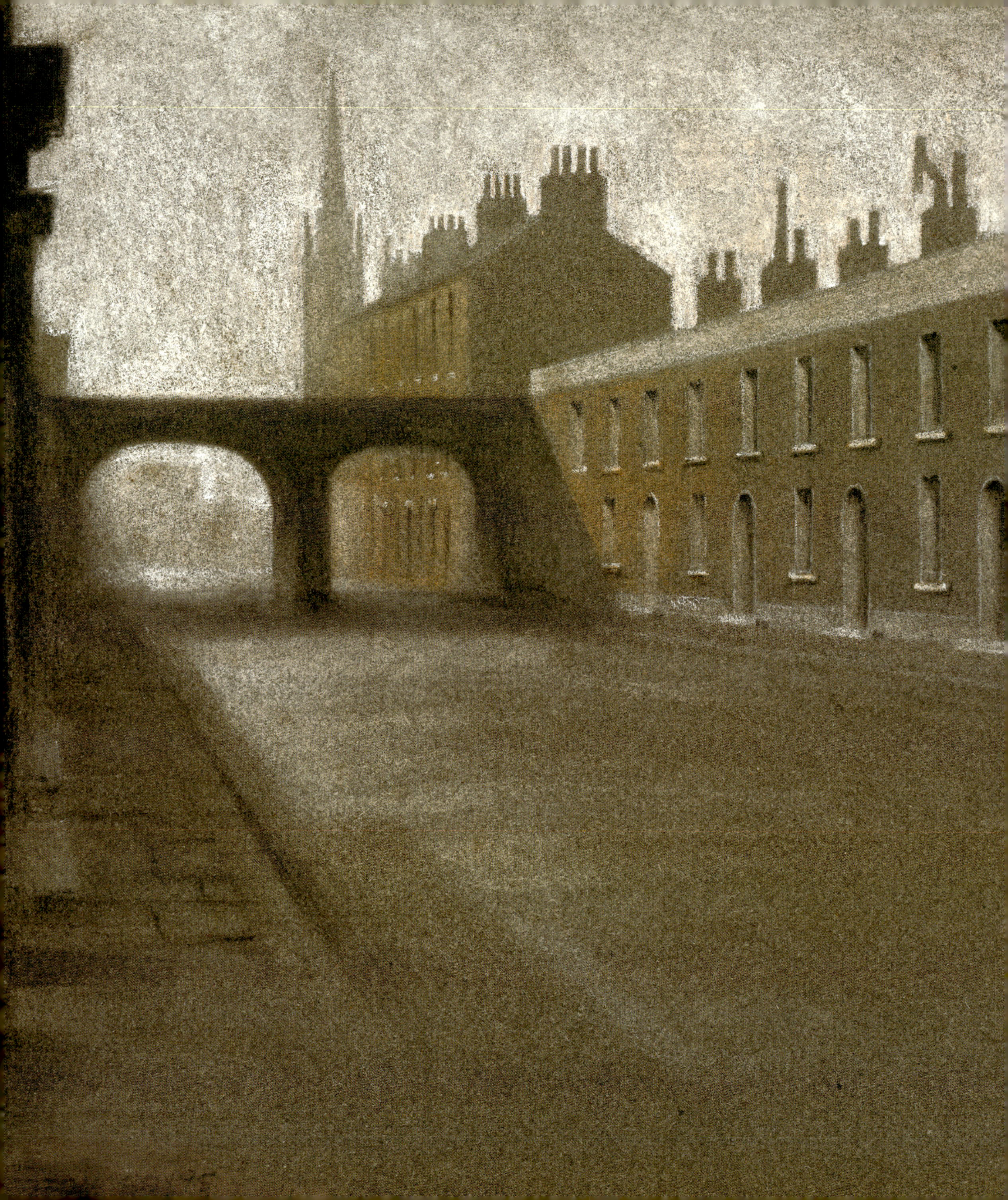

Townscapes

If buildings of all kinds are at the heart of Falcon's desire to document change, there is nowhere they come together in more rich and interesting ways than industrial townscapes. Towns were transformed by the Industrial Revolution. New towns were created by industry, many existing towns grew into straggling built-up areas, and there was a great rebuilding as new commerce and population growth brought investment and changing needs for accommodation. Newport in south Wales was one example, a medieval port that became a thriving industrial borough. Wealth from trade in coal and iron brought from the valleys to the north in the late eighteenth and early nineteenth centuries created a thriving place of good Georgian houses and busy river quays, and Victorian growth continued the prosperity as Newport became a railway port with suburbs, parks and civic buildings. Newport also experienced the post-industrial desolation and intensive redevelopment that affected many townscapes in the mid to late twentieth century and drew Falcon to document them.

The profusion and interrelationships of buildings in towns show up small details of the local vernacular – materials, building forms, layouts – that come together with the evolution of the settlement, to create what we nowadays call distinctiveness. Many people miss what Falcon sees as the beauty of industrial towns like Blaenau Ffestiniog, but he has helped open many eyes to its architectural consistency as a Victorian working town dominated by slate, its extraordinary setting amid waste tips and mountains, and the comfort with which houses, chapels, shops, railways and roads nestle together. His drawings of Blaenau celebrate more than anything how 'real' it is. He has often been more interested in the backs of buildings, irregular, full of life and telling stories, than better ordered frontages. He draws façades too, but it is round the back that one senses Falcon really likes to delve, finding the 'other' townscape. His Worktown project has honoured 'the British nineteenth-century industrial town, and the social revolution that transformed our lives'. He calls it 'a Fanfare for the Common Man'.[13]

Sunday morning, Stepney, 1975 (detail)

The quietness of this empty street in London's East End and the hazy light giving way to the early morning create a ghostly air. The picture recalls days before cars were parked on every kerbside and when shops and workplaces were nearly always closed on Sundays. The church spire and the railway bridge dominate the scene of regular, ordered housing.

Chalk on paper, 46 x 46 cm. FHA 03/93

Rhiwbryfdir from Holland's level, Blaenau Ffestiniog, 1997

This composite of views of Glanypwll Road in Rhiwbryfdir, Blaenau Ffestiniog, includes elevated perspectives from the nearby Holland's Level slate tip. It shows how the houses, shops and chapels nestle comfortably together despite their haphazard development, and how the frontages belie the intensive exploitation of rear plots for further buildings. The drawing centres on Rhiw Calvanistic Methodist chapel: first built in 1856, the chapel was indeed central to community life.

Pencil, ink and watercolour on paper, 28 x 63 cm.
FHA 01/013 - NPRN 305760 and NPRN 8407

67 High Street – four views, Four Crosses, Blaenau Ffestiniog, 2001

This image composites four different views of number 67 High Street, Blaenau Ffestiniog. The drawings set number 67 in the context of the surrounding town, showing how one building fits into the townscape, and in doing so makes the viewer aware of the importance of each building's contribution to the overall character of the town. In the distant view of the townscape number 67 is just right of centre, facing the great rock across the road.

Pencil and watercolour on paper, 21 x 29.5 cm. FHA 01/056 - NPRN 8378

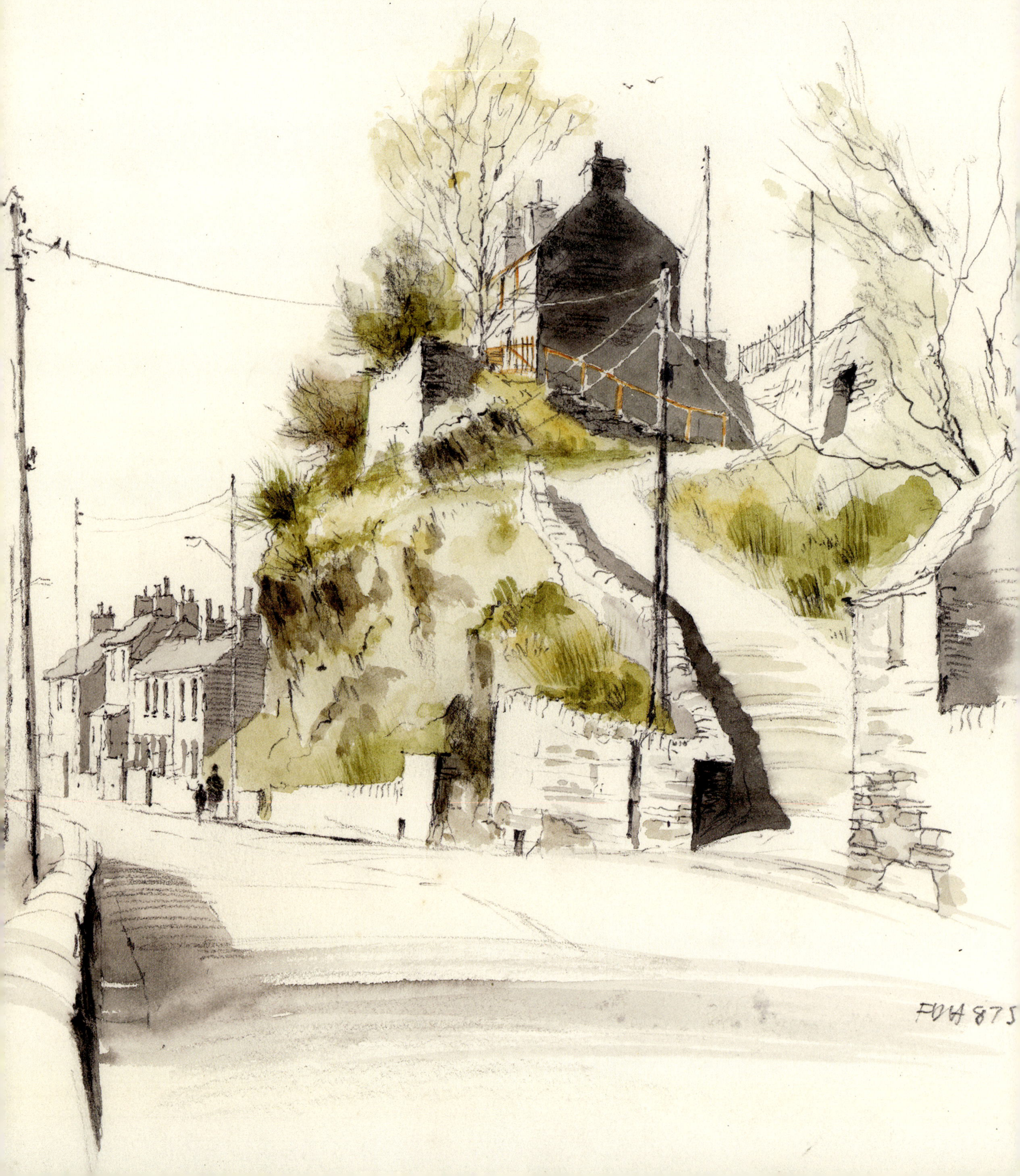
FDH 87S

Level crossing, Blaenau Ffestiniog, 1969

The higgledy-piggledy character of Blaenau Ffestiniog, a townscape that grew up in the spaces between transport routes, quarries and tips, was part of what attracted Falcon to live there. This was among his earliest drawing of the town. The level crossing in Blaenau Ffestiniog was built to accommodate a new branch line of the Ffestiniog railway for the quarries on the east of the town. The line later became the main one into the town. This drawing shows the original gates, each supported by stays from tall gateposts. These were later replaced during modernisation works by standard automatic flashing lights.

Ink and watercolour on paper, 15 x 32.5 cm. FHA 01/122 - NPRN 416064

Pant-y-Celyn, end view from road, 1987

Pant-y-Celyn in Tan-y-grisiau, Blaenau Ffestiniog, is a workers' cottage built close to the Ffestiniog railway, which runs along the rear of the property. The house perches atop a rocky outcrop and is accessed up a steep track. The drawing emphasises how domestic buildings fit into the industrial landscape.

Pencil and watercolour on paper, 20 x 21 cm.
FHA 01/096 - NPRN 417366

Morgan Arcade, Cardiff, 1987

This drawing of the Morgan shopping arcade in Cardiff city centre is a preparatory sketch for a drawing that appeared in Falcon's Cardiff exhibition in the late 1980s. Morgan's Arcade was built in about 1896. Others were built later and Cardiff is still known as a city of arcades. The complex geometry of the curving covered street and its glazed roofs is made particularly clear in this line drawing.

Pencil on paper, 59 x 42 cm.
FHA 02/55 - NPRN 31886

Prince of Wales theatre and the Philharmonic, Cardiff, 1986

This sketch on a scrap of paper shows the clustered buildings at the southern end of Cardiff city centre, close to the central station. The Prince of Wales theatre and the Philharmonic music hall meet in the block, with pubs and shops filling the corner and brewery chimneys rising behind. Falcon notes that while the buildings may appear to be worn they are nonetheless 'vibrant with detail, texture and life', forming an important part of the character as well as the physical townscape of the city.

Pencil and watercolour on paper, 8.5 x 14 cm. FHA 02/77 - NPRN 31871

Overton-on-Dee, A Sketchbook with Comments by Falcon D. Hildred, 1992

Artwork for the front cover of Falcon's sketch book about Overton-on-Dee near Wrexham in north Wales. It echoes a book Falcon grew up with in his home, Joseph Pike's Chester: A Sketchbook. The publication is an annotated guide to the townscape, and includes suggestions about redevelopment.

Pencil and watercolour on paper, 42 x 30 cm. FHA 02/63 - NPRN 305580

The 'Old Co-op', as it is known, on the corner of Pen-y Llan Street and Church Road, is one of my favourite buildings in Overton, and as I have already said, it is a vital cornerstone in the layout of the village. It is very good architecturally, and with its neighbours and wall with acorn pillars, forms a most attractive group. Only the bay windows, which must be later additions, are wrong. There are rumours that it may be demolished, but I've seen buildings in far worse condition restored, and this one really *must* be.

We can learn a lot from the wall with the acorn pillars. When we build a wall nowadays, we simply make it long enough and high enough to do the job. We then stop laying bricks and that's the end of it. But this wall uses the third dimension of depth or thickness, and it's this that makes it so much more attractive. It's thick at the bottom in order to bear the weight and provide a sound footing, and gets thinner in stages as it increases in height in order to reduce weight and materials — all very practical and cost-effective. It's then topped by a generously projecting coping supported on a course of dentilled headers,* all of which creates a simple yet very strong and pleasing pattern of light and shade. So in using the third dimension of depth, the builder is also making use of light. By not doing the same, we reduce the interest and pleasure of our work by as much as one third! It saves cost, but that's all you can say for it. Which wall would you prefer? I never tired of walking past this one.
As I keep saying, these days we neglect beauty. We save on aesthetics in order to pay for the practicalities. So instead of doing a little and doing it well, we do a lot badly. It gets more done, but it leaves a feeling of meanness. Maybe this is why plain walls tend to attract graffiti. A plain wall is mere building, whereas the acorn wall is architecture ~ a perfectly harmonious balance of usefulness and beauty; something that has turned the problem to advantage and thereby enhances our surroundings. There's no feeling of meanness about this wall. We feel, rather, that we have been well treated. That's good design.   * See page 11

A scheme for restoration :—
By replacing each of the bay windows with either one or two sash windows in keeping with those on the first floor, the central entrance would again project forward and therefore regain its former prominence. The areas left by the bays could then be planted up with appropriate climbers such as Clematis, Wisteria and Virginia Creeper. With the carpark adjoining, it would make an ideal public building.

Overton-on-Dee, 1992

Gwydr House or the 'Old Co-Op' as it is known locally, is on the corner of Church Street and Pen-y-Llan Street in Overton-on-Dee. Falcon describes it as one of his favourite buildings in Overton and discusses the possibility of removing the two projecting bay windows at ground floor to allow the central projecting entranceway to stand proud as originally intended.

Pencil and watercolour on paper, 42 x 30 cm. FHA 02/63/13 - NPRN 305580

Suggitts Lane and big dipper, Cleethorpes (Grimsby), 1976

This drawing of the beach at Cleethorpes, Grimsby, illustrates the town where the artist would spend time as a child before he moved to Coventry. The townscape is dominated by the pleasure beach in the background and a steam train leaving passengers. Unusually, Falcon has included a group of people in the image, expressing their enjoyment of the place even on a winter day.

Ink, watercolour and candle wax on paper, 9.5 x 28 cm. FHA 03/09

Wivenhoe, Essex, 1979

A view of Wivenhoe in Essex, from the other side of the estuary of the River Colne, showing the town's waterfront buildings and vessels moored against the quay. This was intended as a preliminary study but Falcon took it no further. The river frontage continues to be busy with the activity of boating.

Ink, watercolour and candle wax on paper, 26 x 103.5 cm. FHA 03/04

Wivenhoe, Essex. Falcon D Hildred 24 Nov '89

2-18 Lansdowne Lane, London, 1967

This drawing shows a typical row of terraced housing in London from an elevated perspective that reveals the layout of small street frontages and long, narrow gardens behind that taper to almost nothing.

Pencil on paper, 10 x 10 cm. FHA 03/36

Spuds, Birmingham, 1979

The townscape is made up of transient objects as well as buildings. Falcon came across the mobile stove cart of a baked potato and chestnut vendor on Fox Street in Birmingham. He expresses his delight in it by views from several different angles, annotations and sketched details.

Ink and watercolour on paper, 19 x 18 cm. FHA 03/65

BAKED
POTATOES

CHESTNUTS
25P
A BAG

outside
Fox Street depot,
B'ham.

FHM Jan 79

BAKED
POTATOES

CHESTNUTS
25P
A BAG

SPUDS
20P

CHESTNUTS
25P A BAG

SPUDS
20P

hot stove →
baking drawers
fire →

Farr & Reddy, Coventry, 1967

This drawing of The Farr & Reddy grocery shop, off licence and bakehouse in Coventry shows a traditional late nineteenth- and early twentieth-century shop front, together with a side elevation of the warehouse and storeroom behind. The character of such shops is conjured in the details of signs for Hovis bread and Mitchells & Butlers Ales & Stouts. The middle drawing records the common sight of windows blanked out with whitewash

Pencil and watercolour on paper, 28 x 18.5 cm.
FHA 03/66

Deptford Mill, London, 1978

Market stalls, shops, flats and an industrial building cluster together in this section of London urban landscape. The J. & H. Robinson flour mill and warehouse at Deptford Mill in London rises above a row of shops and stalls in the foreground. The Robinson flour mill was built in the 1820s and was connected to the Thames by a tidal dock, which meant that the wheat could be bought directly to the mill on barges and flour could be exported the same way.

Pencil and watercolour on paper, 22 x 21 cm. FHA 03/71

Eastport, Falkland

Falcon D Hildred 84

Eastport, Falkland, Scotland, 1984

This study takes in the townscape at Eastport in Falkland. Vernacular buildings sit comfortably alongside more universal styles, showing the townscape as a composite but complementary set of buildings.

Pencil and watercolour on paper, 21 x 33 cm.   FHA 04/06

Fife, Scotland – buildings with man on bike, 1984

The keenly observed roofline of these buildings in Fife shows the crow-stepped gables evocative of houses in the Low Countries and emphasises the long cultural as well as economic connections between the east of Scotland and other nations.

Pencil and watercolour on paper, 22 x 38 cm. FHA 04/08

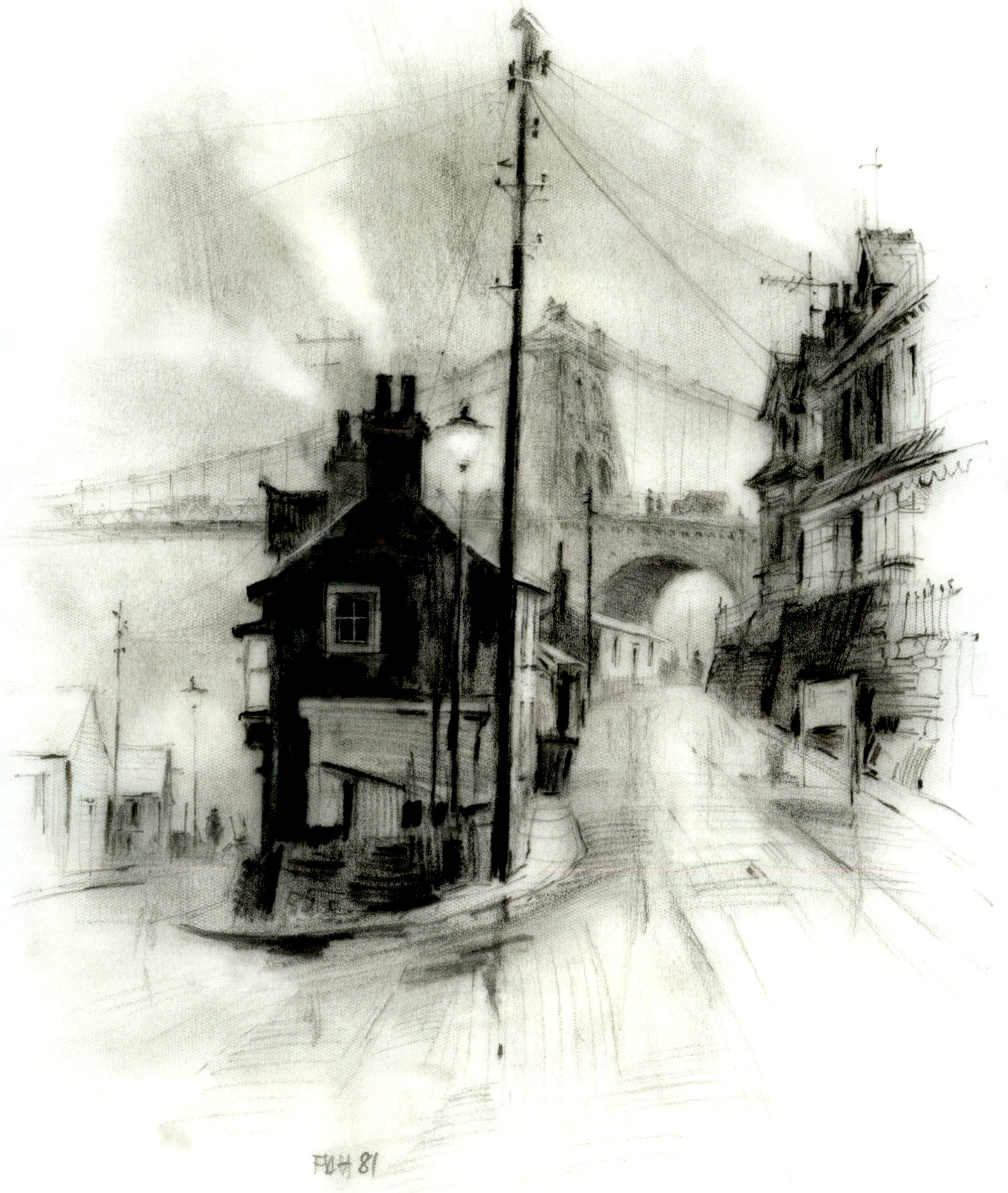
FDH 81

Llanwern steelworks and Corporation Road school, 1988

Llanwern steelworks was the first oxygen-blown integrated steelworks in Britain when it opened in 1962 on green-field land east of Newport. It was an addition to Newport's heavy industries and joined the industrial townscape at a distance above the rooftop of Corporation Road school and streets of housing. In 1988, the 'heavy end' of the works was still in operation. However, this ceased in 2001 and many of the buildings on the site were demolished shortly afterwards. The drawing provides a record of town and steelworks on the cusp of a wave of industrial change that affected Britain from the late twentieth century.

Watercolour on paper, 48 x 73 cm. NPMG.1992.37 - NPRN 86821
Reproduced with permission of Newport Museum and Art Gallery

Menai Bridge at dusk, 1981

This drawing captures well the way in which Telford's suspension bridge across the Menai Strait looms over the townscape of the settlement that grew up next to it, known itself as Menai Bridge. The view is taken from the corner of Beach Road (on the left) and Cambria Road. The artist takes a delight in the higgledy-piggledy clutter of the town, contrasted with the strength of the great bridge.

Pencil on tracing paper, 19 x 16 cm.
The Ironbridge Gorge Museum Trust, Telford Collection: IGMT.2011.785 - NPRN 268065

Weighbridge, Cardiff Road, 1988

This weighbridge on Cardiff Road in Newport measured the weight of loads carried by lorries and wagons. The weighbridge plate is set into the road surface in a street of houses with the small weighman's office to its left. The positioning shows how heavy industry and transport was integrated fully with the townscape and the everyday lives of people in Newport.

Watercolour on paper, 28 x 58 cm. NPMG.1992.38 - NPRN 301223
Reproduced with permission of Newport Museum and Art Gallery

Bellevue Park, 1988

Paradoxically, industrialisation gave rise to green spaces as well as taking them away. As urban centres developed and expanded, municipal leaders became aware of the need to provide open spaces for people to enjoy. During the nineteenth century, parks like Bellevue in Newport developed to provide spaces for exercise, fresh air and relaxation away from the noise and bustle of the industrial town around it.

Watercolour on paper, 55 x 38 cm.
NPMG.1992.44 - NPRN 266093
Reproduced with permission of Newport Museum and Art Gallery

The Pavilion Gardens

The manmade cascade & some of the 500 species of plants & trees

Victorian & 30's pavilions & the adventure playground of 1982

Almshouses overlooking the park

Glazed tile drinking fountain (now broken) presented to the town in 1913 by The British Womens' Temperance Association

Bellevue Park, Newport

Prospect of Newport, 1988

Falcon conveys the sense of Newport as a constantly evolving townscape in this amalgam of images that capture the many aspects of the town and tell its story, from the digging of its canal in the Industrial Revolution to its proud Victorian rebuilding and its most recent architecture. The artist's commentary makes clear his feelings about the character of Newport and how it has changed.

Watercolour on paper, 42 x 30 cm.
NPTMG.1992.69 - NPRN 268069
Reproduced with permission of Newport Museum and Art Gallery

Octopus Bridge, 1988

Falcon's commission from Newport Museum and Art Gallery set out to capture the lesser-known parts of the town as well as its more polite landmarks. The unusually named Octopus Bridge was at the bottom end of Lower Dock Street and had a number of roads leading off it, like the tenticles of an octopus. It was demolished in the 1990s to make way for a new distributor road and roundabout. The name survives as that of the roundabout. The row of buildings survives and several have recently been restored.

Watercolour on paper, 22 x 54 cm. NPMG.1992.55 - NPRN 268069
Reproduced with permission of Newport Museum and Art Gallery

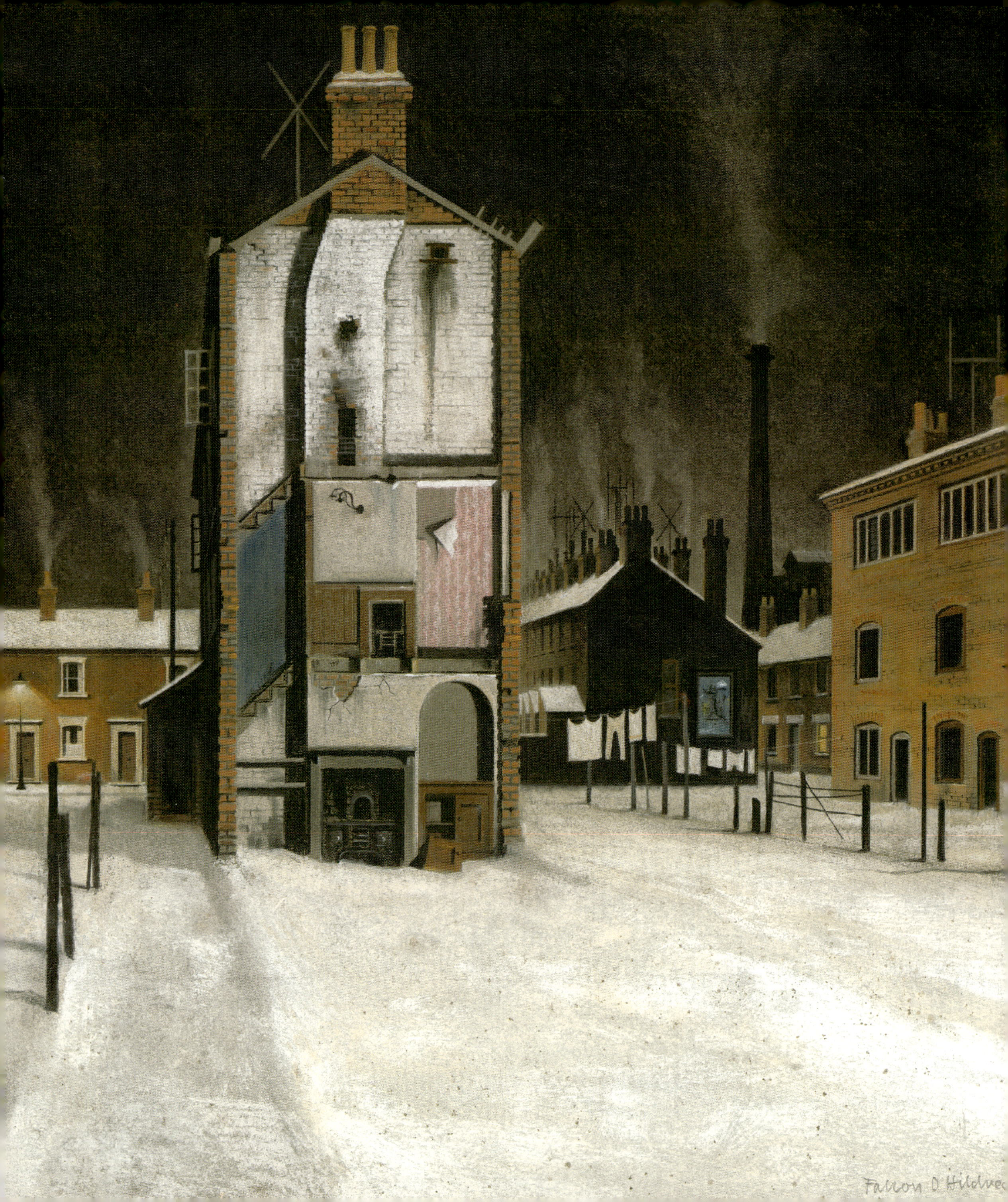

Housing

The Industrial Revolution transformed housing in Britain. Population grew at unprecedented speed across the country but it was especially focused in the industrialising areas. Falcon's recording eye has been focused on the houses of industrial workers in particular, in all their diversity of form and type. Elsewhere, he has documented the cottages of the rural poor, agricultural workers' houses built by the great estates, middle-class housing in nineteenth-century towns and suburbs, almshouses and twentieth-century public housing.

As rural populations migrated to booming centres of heavy industry in search of jobs, new types of housing were created that could accommodate ever-growing numbers of workers and their families close to mines and factories. The belief that buildings are about people is central to Falcon's recording philosophy, and respect for the lives of ordinary people and their unsung contribution has underpinned his work. His meticulous drawings of Tŷ Uncorn record the earliest surviving houses associated with the world-famous slate industry in Blaenau Ffestiniog: he reconstructs them with his characteristic eye for details that might go unseen in a photographic medium and shows how the property evolved through time to meet the changing needs of its occupants.

Falcon captures the boom and bust of industries during the nineteenth and twentieth centuries, for example evoking the sudden depression that affected Eli Green's cottage factory in Coventry. His series of plans, sections and atmospheric sketches of this complex of housing provides a typically detailed yet simultaneously emotive account of how textile workers in Coventry united their work and home lives.

In the last sixty years there has been another, post-industrial revolution in Britain's housing. Intensive bombing of industrial targets during the Second World War damaged or destroyed many of the nineteenth- and early twentieth-century terraces that had housed the urban working population and provided an impetus for redevelopment fuelled by the desire to raise something new and forward-looking from the devastation. Densely populated terraces such as Lansdowne Lane in London were considered out-dated and were demolished to make way for high-rise developments. Many inner-city families across the country were rehoused in estates of semi-detached suburban homes on green-field land at the city outskirts.

Hertford Square, Coventry, 1975

This drawing shows Hertford Square in Coventry after partial demolition. The buildings were weavers' houses, with workshops on the top floor of the home. The workshop space was painted white, to make most effective use of the light drawn in through the large windows. Falcon noted that demolition might sometimes be in progress for many years, leaving such strange, ghostly sights throughout the city. The remaining houses were occupied by squatters and it was considered a scandal that such squalor could coexist with the post-war boom.

Chalk on paper, 26 x 28 cm. FHA 03/81

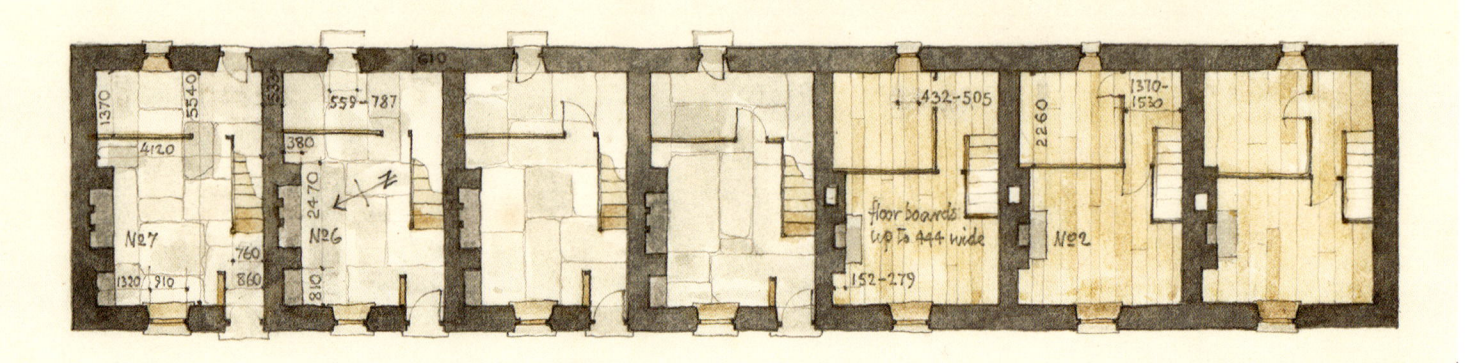

Uwchllaw'r Ffynnon – plan and elevations, 1978

This row of seven workers' cottages in Bethania, Blaenau Ffestiniog, was built in the mid-nineteenth century. The internal division of space on the ground floor in each cottage is similar. The four left-hand houses of the plan show the ground floor covered in slate slabs; the three right-hand houses show the upstairs plan with timbered floors. This drawing is a valuable record of these houses, which were empty and ruinous by 1975. Detailed drawings of features in the houses are on pages 192-93. At the time Falcon recorded them they had been condemned, but Falcon sought their listing and they are now lived in again.

Pencil and watercolour on paper, 18 x 18 cm. FHA 01/111 - NPRN 28882

Managers and the managed, 1999

Industrial development during the eighteenth and nineteenth centuries created a need for varieties of housing that reflected social stratification and the relationships of workers to foremen, managers and owners. This drawing contrasts the housing for the 'managed' quarrymen down in the valley in terraced houses and the 'managers' in larger, detached homes. Falcon notes how the slate roofs seem to merge with the slate tips.

Ink and watercolour on paper, 12 x 29 cm. FHA 01/124 - NPRN 305760

Tŷ Uncorn – view from rear, 1978

The four separate dwellings were later amalgamated into two cottages: one facing east, the other west. The entrance and outbuildings associated with the west-facing cottage are visible in this drawing. The terraced housing more typical of most industrial towns is seen in the background.

Pencil and watercolour on paper, 21 x 23 cm. FHA 01/142 - NPRN 28880

*Tŷ Uncorn –
view from gate*, 1978

Tŷ Uncorn is one of the oldest surviving domestic buildings associated with the slate industry in Blaenau Ffestiniog, built in about 1810 by Lord Newborough to house workers. Four dwellings clustered around a shared central chimney stack. The name means One-chimney House, from the Welsh word for unicorn but it is also sometimes called Inkpot House owing to its similarity of shape to an old glass ink bottle. In this drawing Falcon has included a sheep that has got into the garden and is eating a tree.

Pencil and watercolour on paper, 21 x 18 cm.
FHA 01/141 - NPRN 28880

Tŷ Uncorn – reconstruction of interior, 1978

These drawings reconstruct the interior of one of the four cottages at Tŷ Uncorn. They show how the fireplace – the heart of the home – changed through time. When the cottages were first built, they had traditional open fireplaces which were used for cooking and warming the house. In the mid-nineteenth century, cast-iron stoves were introduced and provided more effective and cleaner ways of heating the home and preparing food. At the time of survey the fireplace had been entirely covered over.

Pencil and watercolour on paper, 21 x 18 cm.
FHA 01/140 - NPRN 28880

Tŷ Uncorn – loft, 1978

This drawing of Tŷ Uncorn shows the loft space above one of the dwellings. It would have been accessed by a wooden ladder leading up from the main ground-floor living area and would have been used for sleeping.

Pencil and watercolour on paper, 21 x 18 cm
FHA 01/139 - NPRN 28880

FDH July 78

Tŷ Uncorn – view through roof, 1978

This drawing reconstructs the interior plans of two of the four separate dwellings at Tŷ Uncorn. On the right, the ground-floor plan of the cottage shows the original open fireplace and stone-flagged floors. On the left, the first floor loft is illustrated, showing how space was partitioned to create a more private sleeping space, which could take advantage of the chimney breast wall warmed by the fire in the room below.

Pencil and watercolour on paper, 21 x 23 cm. FHA 01/143/01 - NPRN 28880

Tŷ Uncorn – extension with chimney, 1978

In the late nineteenth century, a single-storey extension was added to the east side of the building. The extension originally had a very tall chimney, as recorded. This was reduced in height in the late 1990s.

Pencil and watercolour on paper, 21 x 18 cm.
FHA 01/144 - NPRN 28880

Plan of upper floor
No. 1 | 2
3 | 4

Ground floor
← 4420 →

Later addition

FDH 27 June 78 S

'Uncorn', Blaenau Ffestiniog, Gwynedd

Four houses in one. Each house 4420 square inside. Height from ground floor to underside of upper floor 2438. Height from upper floor to torching of roof at eaves 737.

Former Almshouses, Overton-on-Dee, 1992

These former almshouses on Salop Road in Overton-on-Dee near Wrexham were built in 1848 in memory of Caroline Bennion, a daughter of a Wrexham lawyer. Her sisters Dorothea and Mary Ann donated the land, paid for all construction work, and gave an endowment of over £1,000 for the upkeep of the building and care of the residents. The almshouses were occupied by widows over 60 who were resident in Overton-on-Dee and who were members of the Church of England. The buildings have been converted into private homes.

Pencil and watercolour on paper, 10 x 17.5 cm. FHA 02/31 - NPRN 308580

Gorllwyn-uchaf, 2007

This cottage at Prenteg in Caenarfonshire was built in the early seventeeth century. The house stands in upland grazing land and is a cruck-framed hallhouse that was later incorporated into a typical Snowdonian two-unit house. Houses like this are part of the vernacular architectural heritage of Wales.

Pencil, ink and watercolour on paper, 19 x 24 cm.
FHA 02/42/01 - NPRN 404888

Houses on Penhevad Street, 1986

This house on Penhevad Street in Grangetown, Cardiff, was built in the early 1900s and would have provided accommodation for families attracted to the city during its heyday as a coal port, when there were many white-collar jobs as clerks, traders, engineers and merchant navy officers. The house was part of a terrace of similar properties, and is much more architecturally decorative than earlier working-class houses in the city, taking advantage of the supply of cheap, ready-made architectural ornamentation. This embellishment is characteristic of houses built in the city at this time. Since it was drawn, the house has lost its original windows and door and decorated ridge-tiles, and the Pennant sandstone has been painted, but the principal architectural ornamentation survives.

Pencil and watercolour on paper, 24 x 17 cm.
FHA 02/48 - NPRN 301223

Bay Window, Albany Road, Coventry, 1977

The original detail of the bay window on Albany Road in Coventry is preserved in this drawing. The bay window was a popular feature of houses built in the late nineteenth century, providing additional space and light in rooms before domestic gas and electricity supplies provided alternative means of lighting. The drawing records the popular Gothic revival detailing of Victorian suburban middle-class houses, with 'heart and dart' mouldings, scrolls, emphasised keystones and castellation.

Pencil and watercolour on paper, 35 x 27 cm.
FHA 03/11

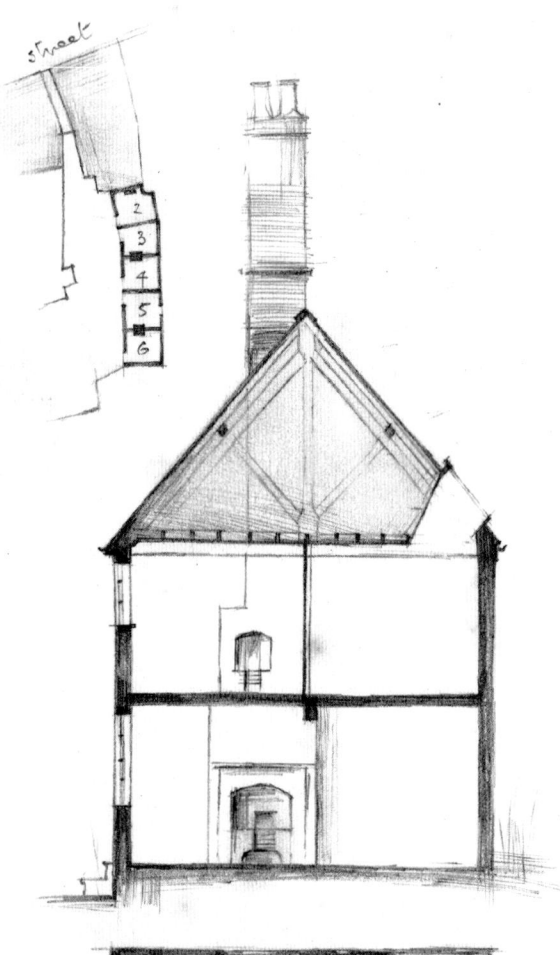

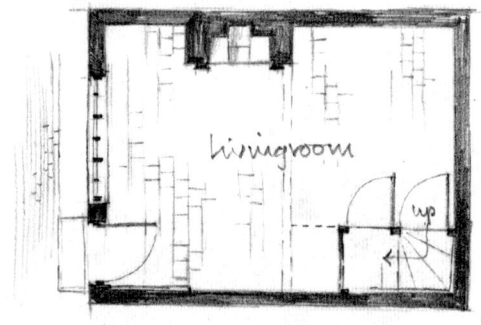

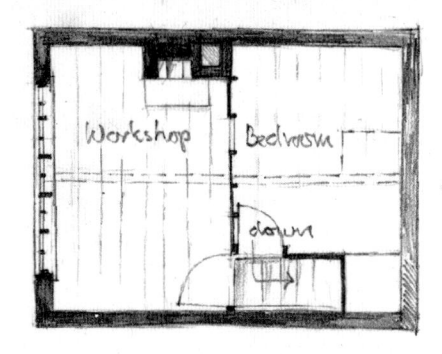

Spon End, Coventry – Tunnel entrance, 1976

Access to the complex of houses and workshops at Spon End was by tunnel-alleys such as this, which gave access to court number 5 on the south side of Spon Street.

Pencil on paper, 19.5 x 11.5 cm. FHA 03/29

Spon End, Coventry – Court 38, 1976

Houses were not only places to live. During the eighteenth and nineteenth centuries, houses were often workplaces too, with families living above shops or incorporating workshops into the home. This plan drawing of Court 38 at Spon End, Coventry, shows a workshop on the second floor of the home above the main living room and adjacent to the bedroom. It was probably used as a weaver's workshop, and had a large window to provide the light needed for textile work.

Pencil on paper, 21 x 9 cm. FHA 03/40

Spon End, Coventry – Court No. 5, 1976

Spon End in Coventry provided both housing and workshop space for textile workers. The large windows shown at court number 5 maximised the amount of daylight for working and are typical of this type of housing.

Pencil on paper,
19.5 x 11.5 cm. FHA 03/28

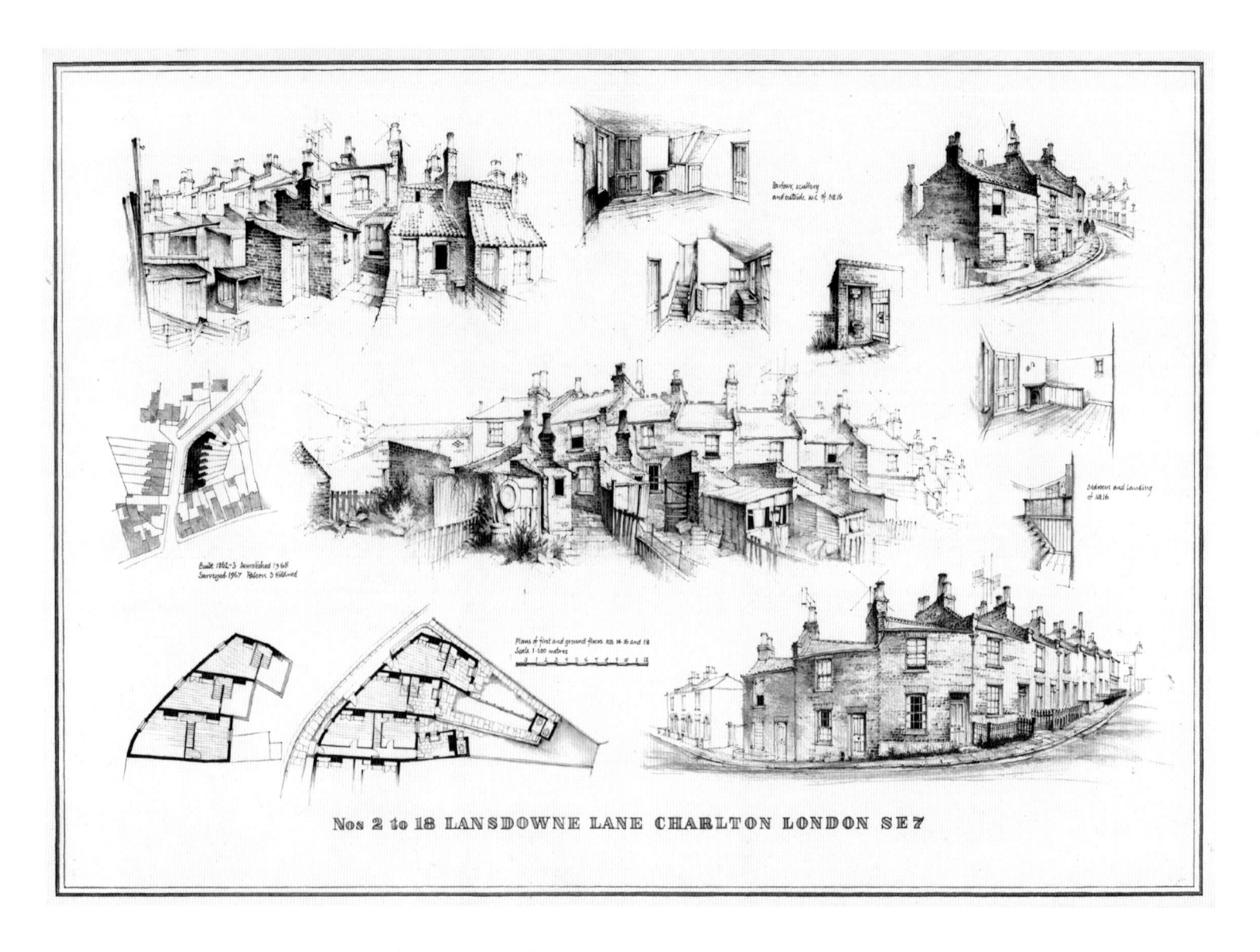

Lansdowne Lane, London, 1970

This prints brings together several drawings to provide a record of the brick terraces that once stood on Lansdowne Lane in Charlton, London. It shows a plan of the street (left), a front view of the houses (bottom right) and a view of the yards and outbuildings to the rear of the property. The drawing also provides a rare record of the houses' interiors. These houses were demolished in 1963 and replaced by multi-storey flats as part of a post-war redevelopment scheme across London.

Print, 59 x 42 cm. FHA 03/06

2 – 18 Lansdowne Lane, London – long front view, 1967

Numbers 2-18 Lansdowne Lane in Charlton provided homes for working-class families. This brick-built terrace swept round a corner site.

Pencil on paper, 15 x 27 cm. FHA 03/38

2 – 8 Lansdowne Lane, London, 1967

Detail of the outbuildings at the rear of Lansdowne Lane in Charlton. These houses were built without bathrooms, with toilets in outbuildings to the rear of each property. The haphazard complex of outbuildings and extensions is characteristic of urban housing in London during the mid- and late-nineteenth century.

Pencil on paper, 12 x 23 cm. FHA 03/20

2 – 18 Lansdowne Lane, London – Living Room, 1967

This drawing preserves by record the interior of one of the terraced houses on Lansdowne Lane. It is not distorted, but shows the unusual shape of the room, fitting into a curved plot, as recorded in the plan on page 90. Many nineteenth-century terraces in London were demolished or extensively renovated during the post-war period as local authorities sought to improve on living conditions they perceived as outmoded, overcrowded and unhealthy. Drawings such as this are an important witness to almost entirely lost characteristics of Britain's built heritage.

Pencil on paper, 11 x 11 cm. FHA 03/33

111 Prospect Vale, London – front, 1975

Number 111 Prospect Vale in Charlton, London, is one house in a terrace, built around the end of the nineteenth century. These houses provided accommodation for middle-class families and are typical of the leafy gardens and spacious homes to which many people at the time aspired. The beautiful frontage concealed a dreadful plan that tapered to the back like a slice of cake. The houses have been demolished and replaced by public buildings. Falcon often used a drawn mount and lettering as part of the image at this time. He realised afterwards that he had made a mistake positioning the chimney on the left with smoke coming out of it, which would have been on the stairs.

Ink and candle wax on wrapping paper, 24 x 37 cm. FHA 03/68

Design work – Clifton Hill, London, 1984

This drawing shows proposed improvements to a house in Clifton Road in the City of Westminster. It was unusual for Falcon to draw higher-status houses in London as they were not under threat in the same way. Late Georgian houses like these invariably have been altered since they were first built to suit the demands of modern living, but sensitive improvements in many cases have allowed their character to be preserved.

Colour prints, 30 x 21 cm. FHA 03/77

Gloddfa Ganol cottages – outhouses and yard, undated

Gloddfa Ganol cottages near Blaenau Ffestiniog, Merioneth, were built in about 1840 for the foremen and clerks employed at the nearby Holland's slate mine. The outhouses and yard depicted here show that some facilities were shared between different families: notably a toilet and a water tap. Shared utilities remained common in isolated housing like this and were the norm everywhere until the introduction of mains water, gas and electricity supplies to towns.

Pencil, ink and watercolour on paper, 30 x 21 cm.
FHA 01/063 - NPRN 302225

Nos 1 to 3 Gloddfa Ganol.
Drawing No 5 of 5
Out-houses + yard

Slab + cement roof

Chemical toilet with vent. Probably shared.

gutter lining

gutter

Oven + water supply in out-house of No. 3. Probably shared.

Pages from Design Book, 2001

A layout, illustrated, written and hand-lettered by Falcon for his publication *A Word in Your Eye or What is Design?* These pages summarise developments in housing in Britain.

Pencil, ink and watercolour on paper, 42 x 30 cm.
FHA 07/07/22

Courtybella Terrace, 1988

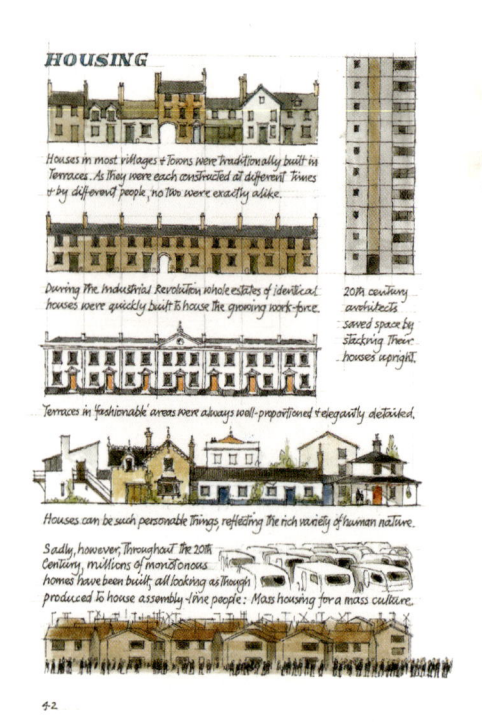

This drawing of Courtybella Terrace in the Pillgwenlly area of Newport was commissioned by Newport Museum, and shows the variety of house designs and styles along one road in the town. Window designs original to the construction of the houses were still in evidence when the drawing was made, but now nearly all have been replaced by plastic windows.

Pencil and watercolour on paper, 21 x 45 cm. NPTMG 1992.39 - NPRN 401103
Reproduced with permission of Newport Museum and Art Gallery

Terrace in Chepstow Road, 1988

This drawing shows the front and rear elevations of a terrace of brick houses at 87-99 Chepstow Road, Maindee, Newport. The ornate frontages contrast with the comparatively plain backs – coloured brick banding and the emphasising of houses at the middle and either end were relatively cheap ways to give some architectural dignity to a terrace. Since this drawing, nearly all of the Victorian detailing has been lost as part of a housing renewal scheme. The chimneys, ornate bargeboards and original windows and doors have been removed and gardens have been replaced by gravelled areas with concrete block walls. The rear elevations have been rendered with pebble-dash and gardens have been concreted for car-parking.

Pencil and watercolour on paper, 21 x 28 cm. NPTMG 1992.40
Reproduced with permission of Newport Museum and Art Gallery

KNOWLEDGE IS POWER

1889

Public and Commercial Buildings

Wherever there are townscapes, public and commercial buildings figure large. Town halls, libraries, schools, pubs, shops, provide the services and facilities that make people come together in urban centres – in many respects they are what towns are all about. The nineteenth century saw a revolution in the range and number of such buildings. Schools and libraries, once the preserve of the few, became accessible much more widely through the work of charitable bodies like the National Schools Society and the trusts that built miners' institutes, and in time through local authority provision. With rising disposable incomes, shops and pubs came to colonise street corners in every new settlement and suburb.

New types of institution required specialist buildings, among them municipal baths, cinemas, department stores and the halls and gyms of the Young Men's Christian Association. These and other public and commercial buildings said much about the aspirations they were designed to fulfil, expressing themselves architecturally as temples of learning, sumptuous emporia or palaces of entertainment.

Since the mid-twentieth century the numbers of such buildings have been on the decline. Changes in mobility and the uses of leisure time – especially as the result of the television and the car – have meant that libraries and institutes have closed, small schools have been replaced, and traditional corner shops have struggled to survive. A few kinds of buildings are now more or less extinct – public wash houses have been made obsolete by domestic plumbing and there are no longer newspaper rooms in libraries where readers stand leafing broadsheets at wooden slopes. Other buildings have been threatened by changing patterns of development and new expectations, such as the expansion of prisons, the mushrooming of out-of-town retail developments and the modernisation of schools and hospitals.

Many of our traditional public and commercial buildings have been vulnerable, but Falcon has captured their qualities when he has seen them under threat. His documentation helps preserve a memory of how former generations sought to improve their living conditions, their comforts or their minds.

Temple Street Library, Newport, 1988

This three-storey library was built in 1889 and dominates the surrounding houses of Temple Street in Pillgwenlly, Newport. It has a rear extension that provides a large, well-lit reading room for users. Public libraries became widespread from the mid-nineteenth century as literacy improved, being provided even in suburbs. The gable bears the inscription 'Knowledge is Power'. The rear view of the property juxtaposes the imposing library building with the comparatively small terraced houses and their vegetable gardens that surround it. The library is still a public building, but as traditional library functions have declined it has become instead a multi-purpose 'community hub'.

Watercolour on paper, 29 x 24 cm. NPTMG.1992.58 - NPRN 268069
Reproduced with permission of Newport Museum and Art Gallery

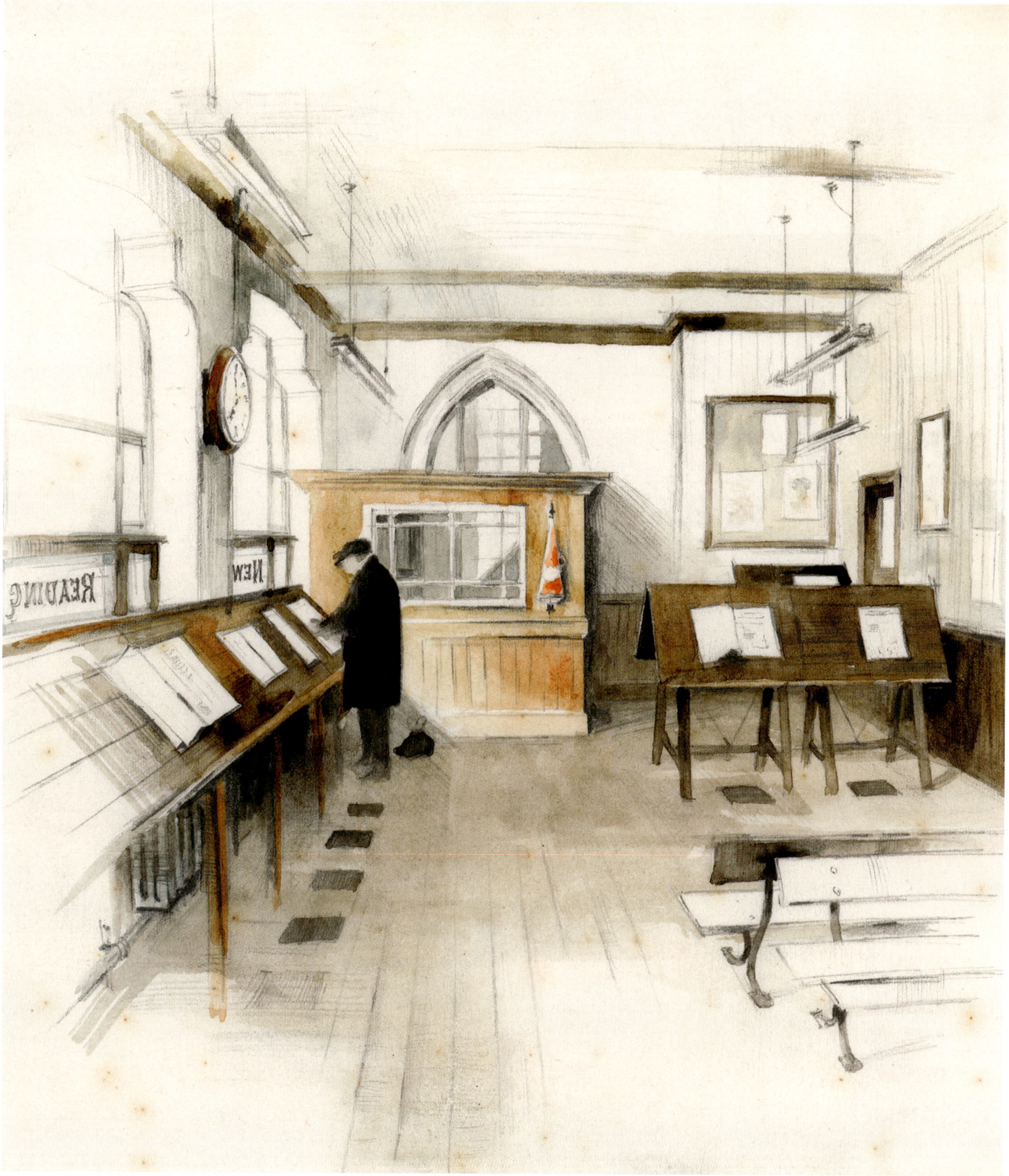
READING
NEW

Newsroom, 1978

In this drawing, Falcon records the reading room at Blaenau Ffestiniog Library. The Arts and Crafts style building, which has gothic-arched doorways on either side of the front elevation, has a balcony and timber-framed oriel windows at first-floor level. The large, ground floor windows seen here provide light for the reading room, where the daily newspapers were laid out on tall, sloped desks, to be read standing.

Pencil and watercolour on paper, 14.5 x 16 cm. FHA 01/110/01 - NPRN 416255

Manod School, 1995

Falcon recorded Manod School at Blaenau Ffestiniog in 1995, presenting several different perspectives of the building in the kind of composite depiction that he has often found to be the best way to summarise a building's characteristics. He captured particularly well the way that the mass was broken up by changes in roof direction. The buildings have since been demolished, apart from the attached teacher's house, which is now a private home.

Ink and watercolour on paper, 18 x 30 cm. FHA 01/130, NPRN 305760

Blaenau – Market Hall and Square, undated

This drawing was made as a preliminary sketch showing a restored Market Square in Blaenau Ffestiniog. The market hall was designed by Mr Owen Morris, an architect from Porthmadog, and was built by a Mr Owen Roberts from Dolgareddu. Constructed from grey stone with red terracotta eaves and a slate roof, it features a projection with a mock balcony that was inaccessible from the interior.

Pencil on paper, 20 x 40 cm.
FHA 01/198/04, NPRN 410658

Prince of Wales theatre, Cardiff, 1986

A site sketch of the Prince of Wales in Cardiff, a popular theatre close to Cardiff Central railway station. The drawing shows the elevation to Wood Street. Built in 1878, it was an exuberant Venetian Gothic design with tall arches to the grand first floor. The interior was subdivided in the late 1980s and the front canopy was removed, but many of the original spaces were sympathetically restored in 1999 when it became the Prince of Wales pub.

Pencil and watercolour on paper 23 x 37 cm. FHA 02/07 - NPRN 3187

The Angel, Newport, 1998

The Angel public house in Newport uses a corner site between West Street and Blewett Street: a curved façade brings the frontage around the road junction, with an entrance on the point of the corner. The pub is at the end of a terrace of houses, and though only a small building it is a focal point for the community.

Pencil and watercolour on paper, 12 x 13 cm. FHA 02/61 - NPRN 300110

Grangetown YMCA, Cardiff, 1986

The Young Men's Christian Association was founded in London in 1844 and originally aimed to provide low-cost housing in a morally safe environment for young men migrating from rural areas to seek work in towns and cities. Falcon recorded the YMCA in Cardiff in 1986, and although the building still stands it is now used as the Grangetown Muslim Cultural Centre. The deep foreground shadow makes this one of Falcon's most dramatic images.

Chalk on paper, 20 x 26 cm. FHA 02/62 - NPRN 310376

Cardiff Prison, 1986

Cardiff prison was commissioned after the earlier Cardiff Gaol was deemed insufficient to cope with the likely prison needs of the rapidly expanding industrial town. It was opened at the end of 1832 with room to house eighty prisoners and twenty debtors. It was built to the 'Pentonville' plan, housed within a seven acre walled enclosure in the centre of Cardiff. Falcon recorded the prison prior to major building works in 1996, when the capacity was increased with the addition of three extra wings. The grey dusk and full moon highlight the myriad lit windows with chilling effect.

Chalk on paper, 15 x 38 cm. FHA 02/66 - NPRN 3072

Emerson Chambers, Newcastle upon Tyne, 1973

This drawing provides a view of Emerson Chambers on Blackett Street in Newcastle upon Tyne, as seen from the foot of Grey's monument. The building originally housed a restaurant, shops and offices. It was built in 1903 to designs by architect Benjamin Simpson, who used the inventive 'Free Style' popular at the start of the twentieth century. It retains its ornate oriels, strapwork and friezes and recently restored art nouveau glazing bars. This area of Newcastle was extensively redeveloped between 1969 and 1976 to make way for the Eldon Square shopping centre. Falcon's drawing, completed in 1973, records the townscape before major construction work was undertaken. He felt that it captured for him something of his excitement at going to Hull for the first time at the age of five and seeing what a big commercial city centre was like.

Ink and chalk and paper, 32 x 23 cm.
FHA 03/10

Icecream man outside school, London, 1977

The black and white pencil work gives depth to this scene, showing children leaving the grand London school at Woodhill in Woolwich and enjoying ice cream from a traditional street vendor. Falcon recalls that seemingly anachronistic scenes such as this were in fact quite common in London during the 1960s and 1970s, though these figures were drawn from childhood memory

Pencil on paper, 18 x 13 cm. FHA 03/23

November home time, Coventry, 1974

This atmospheric drawing shows children at Dover Street School in Coventry, bursting out of school on their way home on a winter's evening in Coventry. The tall Victorian school is warm and welcoming by comparison. The building survives.

Ink and watercolour on paper, 19 x 14.5 cm.
FHA 03/55

Corner Shop, Prospect Vale, Charlton, London, 1976

Small corner shops once served every small group of urban streets, each of them a general store supplying a wide range of household needs. Nearly all disappeared in the late twentieth century. This two-storey building, with double shop frontages and a corner entranceway, is typical. The scene evokes the era of Falcon's childhood in the 1930s, when hand carts were still common on the capital's streets, alongside gas street-lighting, stone pavements and a notable lack of traffic. The large factory chimneys in the background emphasises that this quiet residential scene belies the immense industry of the capital, but the gap to the right was an area of allotments that brought open space into the city. This whole area of nineteenth-century terraced housing in the London Borough of Greenwich was comprehensively redeveloped.

Ink and watercolour on wrapping paper, 26 x 37 cm. FHA 03/70

Municipal Wash-house, Newcastle upon Tyne

Municipal Baths & Wash House, Newcastle upon Tyne, 1976

The municipal baths and wash house in Newcastle upon Tyne were typical of the bath houses built in the nineteenth century. In 1844, the 'Committee for Promoting the Establishment of Baths and Wash Houses for the Labouring Classes' was formed. As a result, in 1846 a bill was introduced that empowered local authorities to fund the construction of these public amenities, giving everyone the chance to wash regularly. Such buildings fell out of use as domestic plumbing became common during the twentieth century.

Pen and ink on paper, 42 x 59 cm. FHA 03/76/01

As Time Goes By, 1988

A street scene in Newport at the east end of Clarence Place is dominated by the vast art deco Odeon cinema, a 'dream machine' designed by Harry Weedon and Arthur J. Price in 1937-38. Britain had over 250 Odeons by the Second World War. The cinema closed in 1981. It was a snooker hall when Falcon recorded it and it is now an evangelical church. The Cenotaph and other buildings also survive, but they are still as cluttered as Falcon depicts them to be here, surrounded by bollards and barriers, cars, and people seemingly dissociated from place. What should have been a respectful public space around the Cenotaph has become in Falcon's eyes a hideous traffic junction. He says, 'This is not what life should be like. This is not what towns should be like.'[14]

Watercolour on paper, 37 x 79 cm. NPTMG.1992.41 - NPRN 603
Reproduced with permission of Newport Museum and Art Gallery

Newport Market, 1988

Newport Market stands on the site that has been used since about 1817 as the town's market. After being extended, demolished and rebuilt again the building has taken on an eclectic mix of styles. The drawing provides a side view, emphasising the large area of ground-floor halls roofed with cast iron and glass, rather than the grand frontage in Upper Dock Street with its tall tower and administrative block in French Renaissance style. Falcon realised that something was missing from the right-hand rooftop and researched it to find there had once been decorative ironwork – he put it back in his drawing. The market has been refurbished and has survived in use.

Watercolour on paper, 64 x 43 cm. NPTMG.1992.51 - NPRN 31986
Reproduced with permission of Newport Museum and Art Gallery

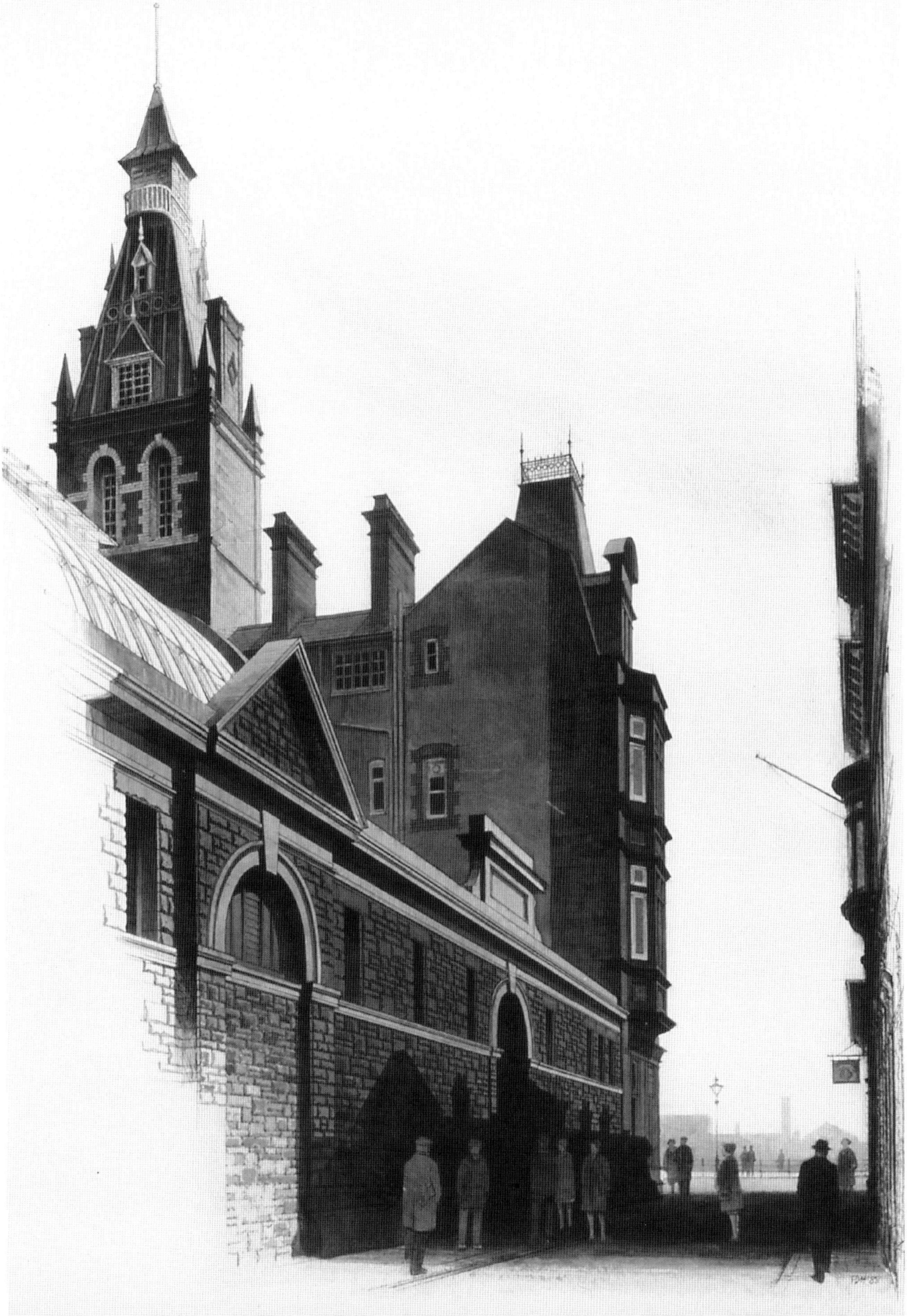

Dockland toilet, Newport, 1988

Public toilets began appearing in large numbers during the Victorian period after The Public Health Act of 1848 called for public conveniences in order to improve sanitation. Architects and engineers were encouraged by local authorities to design them to high standards and civic pride demanded that they were impressive structures. Consequently, they were often built stylishly from materials such as copper, marble and highly decorative tiles. Falcon found this example curiously isolated in a large expanse of empty space at the bottom of Commercial Road in Pillgwenlly. He discovered it had originally stood between six sets of railway lines, crossed by a tram route. It was listed in 1997 and has been restored.

Watercolour on paper, 31 x 34 cm. NPTMG.1992.52 - NPRN 268069
Reproduced with permission of Newport Museum and Art Gallery

Windsor Castle Hotel, Newport, 1988

A three-storey, highly decorated public house that the artist recorded as part of his detailed survey of Newport. The building made good use of a narrow building plot in Upper Dock Street and, like many town-centre pubs, sought to attract customers through stylish and sumptuous architecture and applied art in the form of stone carving, letter cutting, ironwork, joinery and etched glass. It is still in use.

Watercolour on paper, 35 x 21 cm.
NPTMG.1992.57 - NPRN 268069
Reproduced with permission of Newport Museum and Art Gallery

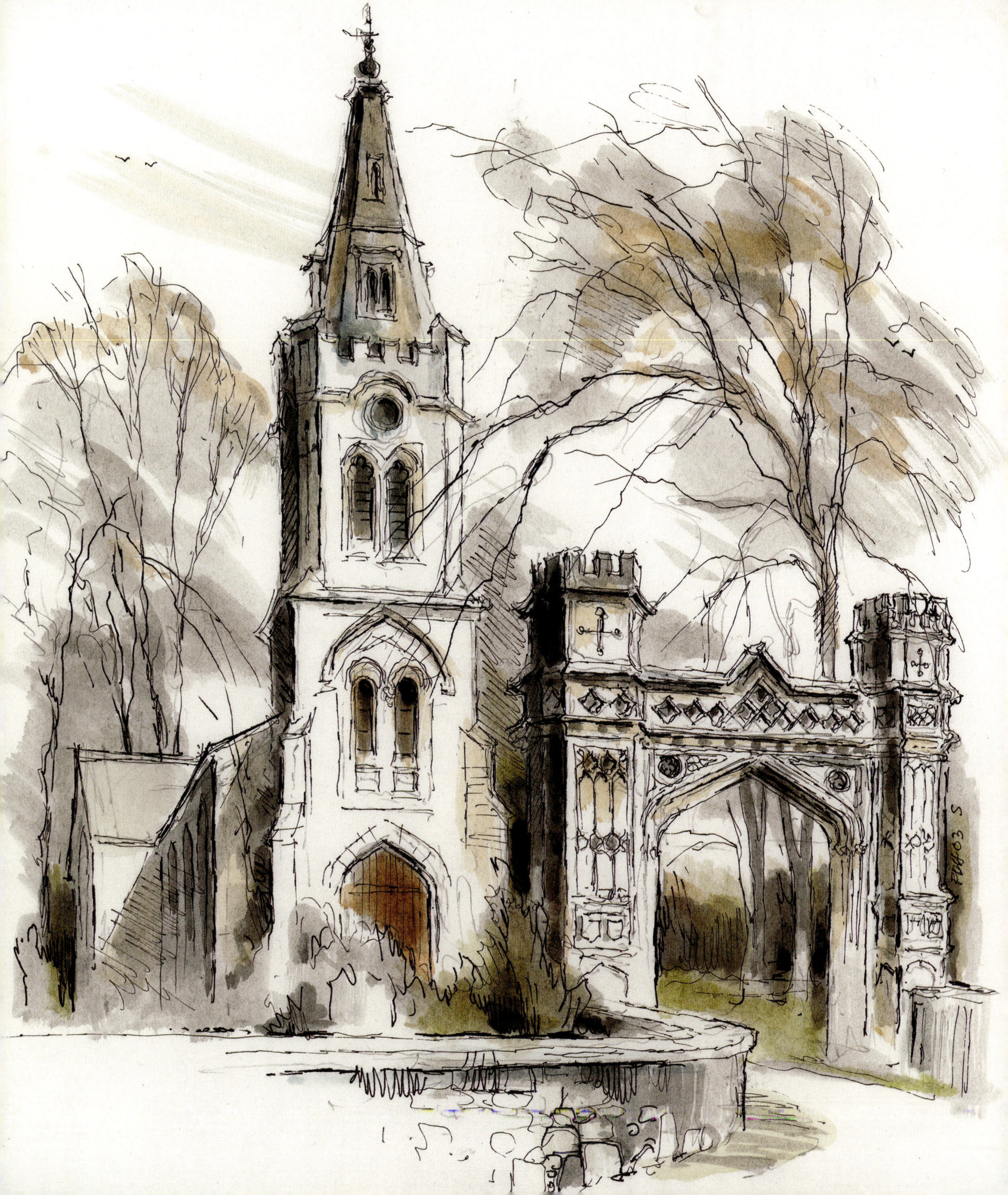

Churches and Chapels

Churches and chapels are among the most prominent architectural components of 'worktowns'. The rapid growth of population in the nineteenth century demanded additional capacity for worship, and the need for buildings was amplified in new industrial towns, villages and suburbs where religious buildings had to be provided for the first time. Tens of thousands of churches and chapels were built across Britain between the early nineteenth century and early twentieth. The fissiparousness of nineteenth-century nonconformist denominations and the enthusiasm of periodic religious revivals made chapels even more numerous.

These new faith buildings represented a huge investment for local communities, and they were justifiably proud of them. Anglican churches like that built to serve the new town of Tremadog might be supported by local landowners and industrialists. Most chapels in industrial areas were built with the aid of financial donations by their largely working-class congregations and often with contributions in kind by way of labour, materials and craftsmanship. This was reflected in the wealth of chapel fixtures and fittings, recorded by Falcon in careful details of pews, pulpits and iron railings. His series of drawings of Bethania chapel in Blaenau Ffestiniog represents one nonconformist building in all its richness.

Such buildings were expressions of architectural aspiration as well as religious fervour, reflecting the Victorian 'battle of the styles', the invention of new hybrid architectural languages or sometimes the untutored vernacular of local designers, builders and ministers. They ranged from the simplest long-wall chapels with minimal detailing to wedding-cake classical temples and complicated Gothic piles. Often they were restyled at various points in their history as they were expanded to cope with larger numbers of worshippers. Ministers' houses, vestries and schoolrooms were also part of this abundant flowering.

Sadly, churches and chapels have been among the most threatened categories of buildings in recent years, particularly those of the nineteenth century in former industrial towns. As congregations have declined, many chapels and churches have closed and have been subject to alterations for new uses of greater or lesser sympathy. Many, too, have fallen into disrepair and finally been demolished. With so many at risk, Falcon's records are important to convey some understanding of these proud expressions of industrial culture to future generations.

Tremadog church and church gate, 2003

One of the earliest Gothic revival churches to be built in Wales, St Mary's was provided by the founder of the planned borough of Tremadog (or Tremadoc), William Madocks MP. A religious liberal, Madocks had to explain to the Bishop of Bangor his decision to provide the town with a nonconformist chapel, stating that the church would be built on stone but the chapel on sand: a true statement geologically. Perched on a prominent rocky outcrop, the impact of the church is enhanced by the Coadestone gateway, which Madocks had shipped from London in kit form.

Pencil and watercolour on paper, 25 x 21 cm.
FHA 02/26 - NPRN 43788 and NPRN 43819

Gwylfa Calvinistic Methodist chapel, Manod, Blaenau Ffestiniog, 1977

Many nonconformist chapels are no longer places of worship. The afterlife of these buildings is varied, but their large internal spaces sometimes invite reuse as workshops. Gwylfa Methodist Chapel in Manod was designed in 1906 by the architect Robert Lloyd Jones of Caernarfon to have a 'show-façade' complete with that iconic element of many gable-ended chapels, the 'Giant Arch'. The impact of the Lombardic style, chosen to distinguish the chapel as much as possible from the domestic and commercial buildings of Blaenau Ffestiniog, has been subsumed by advertising and as the chapel finds new use as a garage and petrol station. It has since been demolished. Falcon refers to the subject as 'St Duckhams' after the oil brand on sale. The drawing was done on site and caught in a rainstorm, so that it had to be recoloured and restretched at home.

Pencil and watercolour on paper, 17.5 x 30 cm. FHA 01/102 - NPRN 8402

Ebenezer Baptist chapel, Plymouth Road, Merthyr Tydfil, 1981

Ebenezer Baptist Chapel in Merthyr Tydfil was built in 1794 and although rebuilt several times it retains the long-wall form and simple architecture characteristic of early nonconformist chapels in Wales. It was built for the booming population working in the iron industries of Merthyr. The railway bridge and water tower came later, so symbols of the two dominant factors in nineteenth-century workers' lives – industry and religion – stood side by side in the streetscape. In 1981 the chapel house bore the iconic advert for Brains bitter, while the inscription still announced 'Capel y Bedyddwyr' – the influence of the teetotal nonconformists had waned. The chapel was disused by 1991 and by 2012 the whole complex had been cleared away.

Pencil and watercolour on paper, 20 x 26 cm. FHA 02/62 - NPRN 9877

FCH 97

English Calvinistic Methodist chapel, Blaenau Ffestiniog, 1997

In Wales, Gothic chapel architecture is traditionally (though often wrongly) associated with English-speaking congregations in otherwise Welsh-speaking strongholds. The rule does hold true of the 'Capel Saesneg' (the 'English Chapel') in Blaenau Ffestiniog. The sum of a hundred intricate details, these sketches record the myriad of mouldings, castings, carvings and forgings chosen by the congregations. The whole effect recalls a nineteenth-century pattern book. The survey was carried out when the use of the chapel was in decline. It occupied a conspicuous point in the street, catching the eye and leading the visitor on, but sadly it has since been demolished.

Pencil and watercolour on paper, 35 x 32 cm. FHA 01/117 - NPRN 8409

*Tabernacl Calvinistic Methodist chapel,
High Street, Blaenau Ffestiniog*, 1974

Tabernacl was the largest and most expensive chapel in Blaenau, seating a congregation of 950 and being valued at £10,790 in 1905. This status is clearly reflected in the grandeur of the classical edifice, which stood on a prominent site, a landmark to the religious fervour of the slate quarry workers and their willingness to fund such remarkable building projects. Falcon says its splendour would have been a credit even to Venice. The drawing emphasises how the triangle of the pediment is echoed by the slate tip on the mountain above, and even the tangle of power lines: the pied architecture of 'worktown'. It was demolished soon after Falcon drew it in 1974.

Pencil sketch on paper, 11.5 x 22.5 cm. FHA 01/89 - NPRN 8410

Havelock Street Methodist church, Havelock Street, Newport, 1992

Falcon shows the Havelock Street chapel as designed in 1878 by Habershon, Pite and Fawkner of Newport. The asymmetry of the main façade is explained by the corner site, but the flanking turrets, wheel window and vibrant colours of the polychromatic stonework produce a strong, Lombardic expression. The matching colours and detail of the adjacent Sunday school belie the ten-year gap between the two buildings.

Pencil and watercolour on paper, 20 x 30 cm. NPTMG.1992.60 - NPRN 10560
Reproduced with permission of Newport Museum and Art Gallery.

Bethania Welsh Independent chapel, Manod Road, Blaenau Ffestiniog, 2001

Bethania was the first Independent chapel established in the parish of Ffestiniog, founded in 1818. The 1839 rebuild was recorded by Falcon in a comprehensive series of drawings. It was later demolished (though the vestry, schoolroom and chapel house remain). The chapel follows the square plan advocated by John Wesley on the basis that it provided the perfect oratory space, in this instance as part of a larger complex of Sunday school, vestry and chapel house. The chapel takes its place among the streets of terraced housing, a reflection that the early nonconformists saw their places of worship as integral to everyday life rather than as buildings to be set apart.

Pencil and watercolour on paper, 16 x 36 cm. FHA 01/21 - NPRN 8369

Bethania Welsh Independent chapel, Manod Road, Blaenau Ffestiniog, 2001

An anonymous actor visiting Wales described the interiors: 'one is aware of the truly dramatic atmosphere of so many Welsh chapels, which like the Elizabethan theatre style, have an intimacy which brings together actor and audience, or pastor and flock, closely locked in the business of drama or worship – or both'. The preaching of God's word was paramount in nonconformist services and the pulpit rather than the altar was therefore the focal point, the layout of ground floor and gallery pews allowing an optimum view for congregation and minister alike. The platform pulpit with its sweeping steps to either side provided the perfect stage for the minister's orations; he was framed by the pulpit arch, and confronted by the gallery clock ticking away the minutes of each carefully prepared act.

Top: Pencil and watercolour on paper, 23 x 36 cm. FHA 01/23,
Middle, left: Pencil and watercolour on paper, 16 x 29 cm. FHA 01/24,
Left: Pencil and watercolour on paper, 16 x 29 cm. FHA 01/22 - NPRN 8369

Bethania Welsh Independent chapel, Manod Road, Blaenau Ffestiniog, 2001

From the austere and simple interiors of the early chapels developed what the Wesleyan Methodists called 'The Age of Mahogany'. Though most of the wood used was pitch pine, clever use of comb-staining and varnishing created rich interiors. Members of industrial congregations often contributed their own skills in carpentry, metal working and masonry and these sketches show the wealth of thought and detail that was put into show pieces and practical objects alike.

Pencil and watercolour on paper, 23 x 29 cm.
Pencil and watercolour on paper, 23 x 29 cm.
FHA 01/25 and FHA 01/26 - NPRN 8369

OPENED 1820

THOMAS TELFORD
ENGINEER
BORN 1757 DIED 1834

Transport and Engineering

Achievements in engineering, especially those concerned with transport, were among the wonders of Britain's industrial era. Many of the heroic civil and mechanical engineering pioneers remain famous today – Telford, the Stephensons, Brunel, Armstrong. Other solvers of engineering problems were seldom well known, but their contributions were all-important in keeping trade and people in motion: they created the culverts that carried quarry tramways over rushing mountain streams, the cranes that lifted goods onto ships, the lock gates that kept the canals in business, the grilles that strained the water people drank.

The scale of the achievements in engineering between the early Industrial Revolution and the twentieth century seems hard to believe. Nearly 1,200 miles of canals were dug in the first twenty years of the canal-building mania, all with picks and shovels rather than machines. Thousands more miles of standard-gauge railways were built, linked to narrow-gauge railways and arterial tramways in factories, mines and quarries that even reached inside buildings and far underground. Sewer systems, steam ships, innumerable locomotives, vast acreages of docks, all appeared during the nineteenth century.

Falcon has drawn some of Britain's engineering masterpieces, such as Thomas Telford's Menai Bridge and Jesse Hartley's Albert Dock, but other artists have captured those, beginning when they were under construction. As a result, Falcon has been more often concerned to document the nitty-gritty of transport and engineering: the infrastructure in daily use. He therefore shows the Menai Bridge not just as a soaring monument but as a working crossing with lorries pressing through its arches, still capable of carrying modern traffic. He records a new concrete viaduct under construction at Newcastle and piles of sand and gravel on the wharf at Newport – such construction processes and working activities are inherently ephemeral but powerfully redolent and informative.

Falcon has been fascinated for many years by the intricate transport interchange at Pant yr Afon near Blaenau Ffestiniog. Here, in a constricted valley head among the slate tips, quarry tramways meet and cross a public railway, a major road swings by and a river passes underneath. All this is managed as a result of a multitude of engineering provisions, including bridges, culverts, a tunnel, inclines, embankments, a crane, sidings and platforms. Such landscapes are full of minor details highly vulnerable to change and decay that together tell a compelling story of engineering achievement and know-how.

Menai Bridge, 1981

Thomas Telford's magnificent suspension bridge was built in the 1820s to carry the Holyhead Road over the Menai Strait. This is not a romantic depiction emphasising the elegance of the structure but a roadway view showing the workaday reality of a bridge still carrying large vehicles and heavy traffic more than a century and a half after it was built.

Gouache and ink on paper, 32 x 25 cm. IGMT.2011.788 - NPRN 43063
The Ironbridge Gorge Museum Trust, Telford Collection

Pant yr Afon – general view from tip, 1969

The nexus of transport routes and engineering features at Pant yr Afon has fascinated Falcon since he arrived in Blaenau Ffestiniog in 1969, though it has changed dramatically in the time since. This view looks down from one of the tips. The central feature is the tramway viaduct that connected Oakley quarry with the Glan y Don slate tip: both viaduct and tip were removed in the 1970s, leaving only the abutment on the right and one pier. The Conwy valley line, still operated by Railtrack, comes out of the tunnel mouth at the bottom of the picture and passes under the viaduct. There are remains of sidings serving Oakley quarry on the right, with a counterbalance incline to the tramway above, and Llechwedd quarry on the left, with a crane for loading. A series of girder bridges cross the river. The Llechwedd hydraulic power house is at bottom left, beneath the A470 climbing the hill towards the Crimea pass.

Pencil, ink and watercolour on paper, 22 x 50 cm.
FHA 01/033 - NPRN 41296 and NPRN 85488

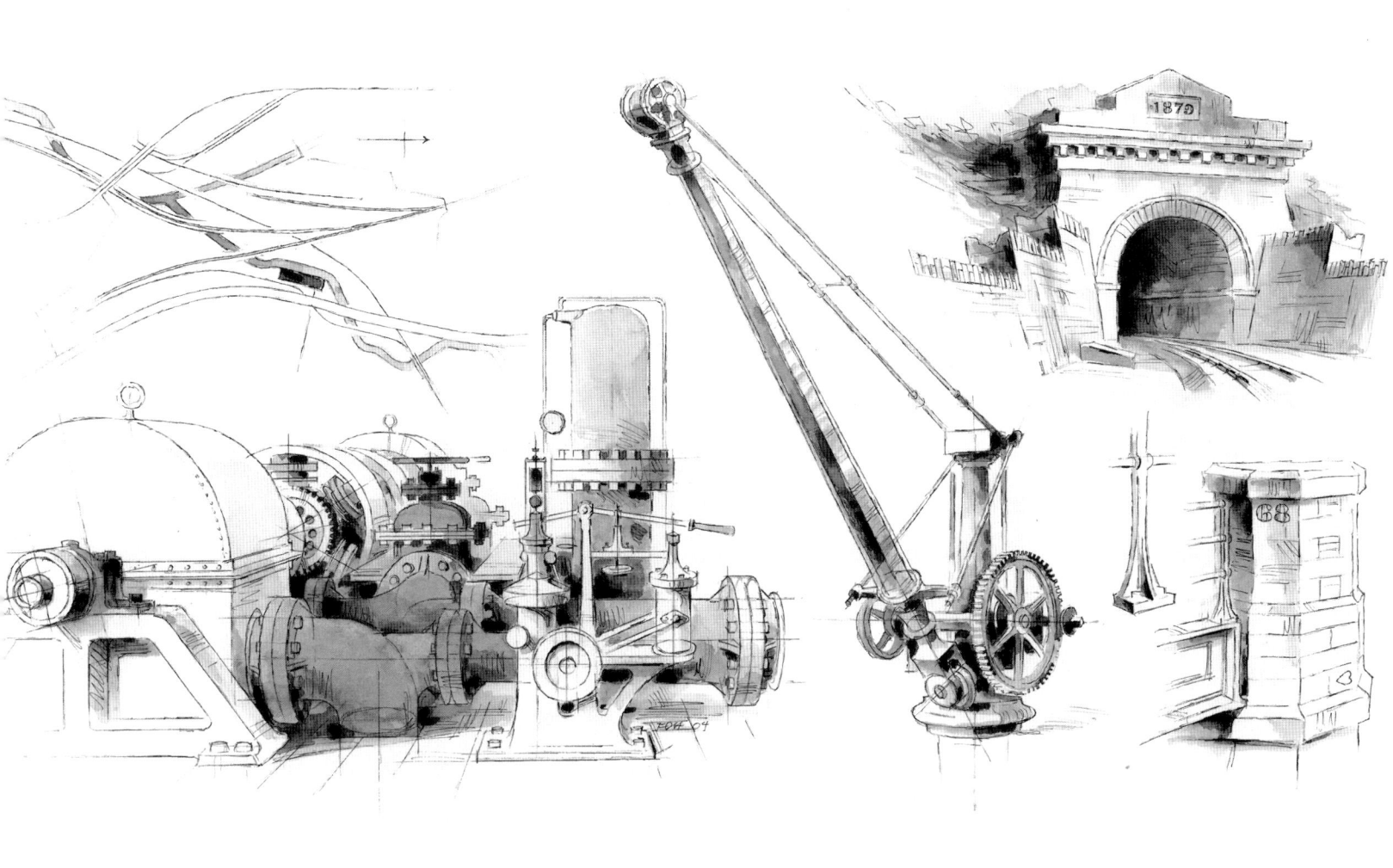

Pant yr Afon – powerhouse and details, 1969

This drawing shows some of the engineering features clustered at Pant yr Afon. The hydroelectric power house was designed to provide a private electricity supply to the adjacent quarries. The drawing in the bottom left shows a Johnson & Philips 175-kilowatt generator, which still operates and now supplies the National Grid. The crane, bridge pier and tunnel portal with the datestone of 1876 were all associated with the railway from Blaenau Ffestiniog through the mountain to the Conwy valley.

Pencil, ink and watercolour on paper, 22 x 40 cm.
FHA 01/032 - NPRN 41296 and NPRN 85488

Llechwedd quarry on the A470, 2005

A drawing of the artist's proposed bridge over the Llechwedd sidings, designed to avoid the northern part of Blaenau Ffestiniog and enable a link with a larger bypass to the west of the town. The bypass had been proposed in 1966 but was never built. Falcon's design is sensitive to the confined location, the character of the existing bridges and the visual connections to be preserved.

Ink and watercolour on paper, 42 x 30 cm.
FHA 01/151 - NPRN 41296 and NPRN 85488

Monoloco, 2008

A drawing of the only working steam monorail loco in the world. Built in 1997 to the design of John Vineers, it was part of the Richard Morris Monorail collection based in Blaenau Ffestiniog.

Pencil, ink and watercolour on paper, 29 x 22 cm. FHA 01/154

MONOLOCO

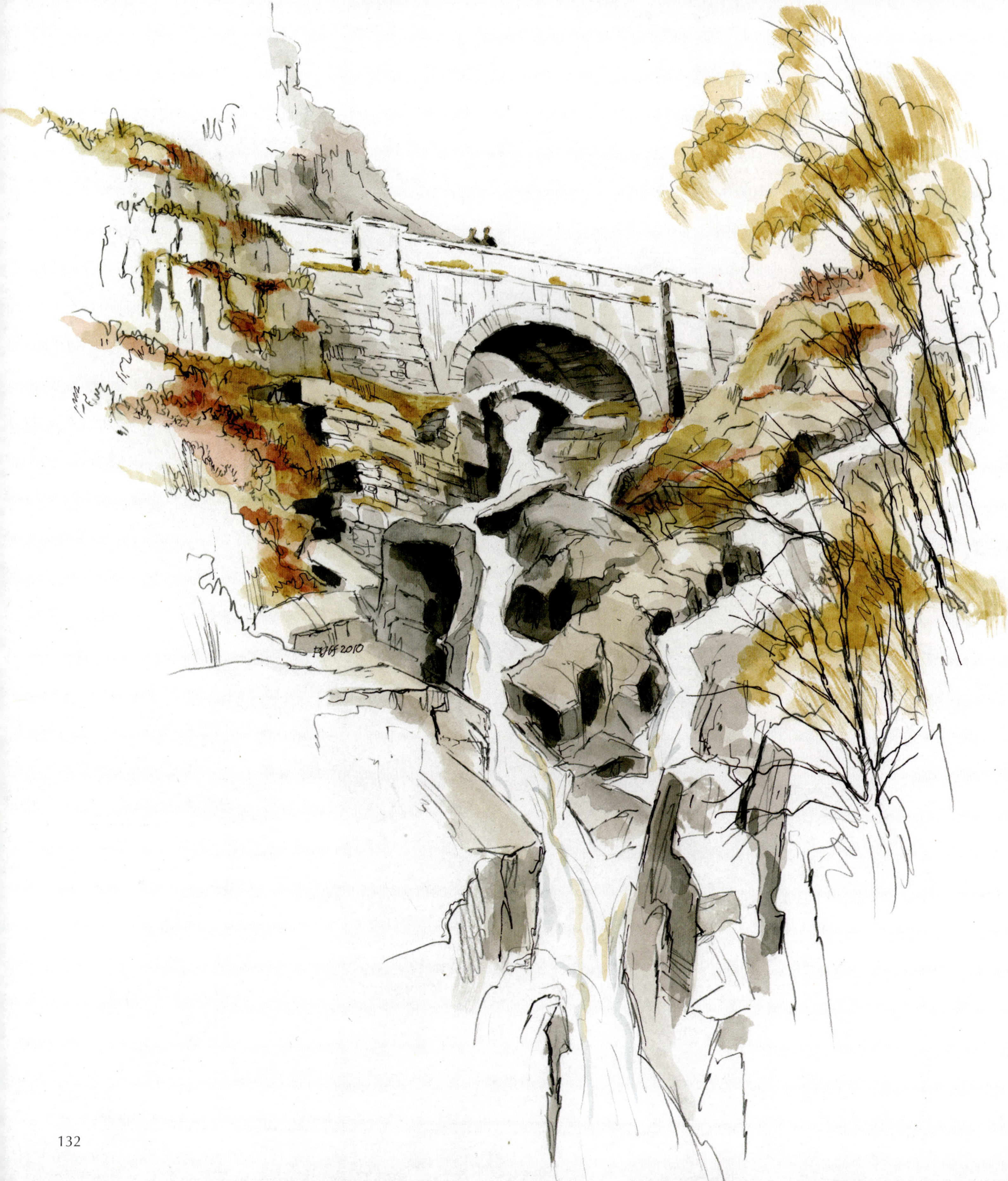

Bridges over Ogwen Falls, 2010

This bridge on the Holyhead road through north Wales was built where the River Ogwen flows out of Llyn Ogwen in an impressive series of waterfalls. It was designed by Thomas Telford as part of his work on the London to Holyhead route in 1815 and is still in use today as part of the A5 through Snowdonia. The drawing shows the fragmentary remains of an earlier bridge, the arch of which was left by Telford underneath his own.

Pencil ink and watercolour, 30 x 27 cm.
FHA 02/13 - NPRN 33022

Vyrnwy filtration tower, 1998

The fairy-tale gothic tower at Lake Vyrnwy in north Wales was designed as part of the reservoir scheme by Liverpool Corporation and was completed by 1890. It is still used for its original purpose as the offtake for the 75-mile aqueduct to Liverpool. A fine steel mesh to filter the water is raised into the tower for cleaning by a small engine.

Ink and watercolour on paper, 24 x 18 cm.
FHA 02/12 - NPRN 32433

Dawn Start – narrowboat at Hawkesbury lock near Coventry, 1975

This drawing reconstructs life on the Coventry canal, showing a horse-drawn canal boat setting off from the busy industrial centre of Coventry in the early hours. During the eighteenth and early nineteenth centuries, canals provided crucial transport links for industries across Britain even after the arrival of the railways.

Chalk and ink on paper, 16 x 26 cm. FHA 03/17

Entrance to Albert Dock, Liverpool, 1975

Liverpool's Albert Dock opened in 1846, designed by the engineer Jesse Hartley (1780-1860). Commercial shipping stopped in 1920 and the warehouses fell out of use in 1972. The drawing captures an atmosphere of past glory and present stillness. By 1982, redevelopment had started under one of Britain's earliest schemes of wholesale adaptive reuse of industrial buildings. The docks are now home to shops, offices, residential areas and the Tate gallery.

Ink and chalk on paper, 17 x 22 cm. FHA 03/44

Building the Metro bridge at Byker 17 Feb 78

Building bridge for Byker Metro, 1978

A snapshot in drawn form of construction in progress for the towering concrete bridge that carries the Tyne and Wear Metro over the Ouseburn. It was opened officially in 1982. The drawing contrasts the ironwork of the railway viaduct beyond, as shown on page 6.

Pencil, ink and watercolour on paper, 36 x 27 cm. FHA 03/64

Humber Ferry, Hull, 1978

One of Falcon's formative memories is of taking the ferry to Hull as a child. The Humber ferries only ceased in 1981 with the completion of the Humber Bridge. The PS Lincoln Castle pictured here was over 200 feet long and one of the last coal-powered paddle steamers in regular service in the United Kingdom. It is currently the focus of a restoration project.

Pencil and watercolour on paper, 14 x 21 cm. FHA 03/72

Port Office and Bailey dry dock, Newport, 1988.

Bailey dry dock closed for ship-repairing business in 2004. It is seen here from East Way road. The dock is still extant, as are most of the buildings in this image, but the black lettering on the walls has faded away and the large crane has disappeared.

Pencil and watercolour on paper, 21 x 83 cm. NPTMG.1992.62.
Reproduced with permission of Newport Museum and Art Gallery:

Moderator wharf from the River Usk, 1988

The wharf gets its unusual name from a boat called Moderator that used to charge 'moderate' rates for shipping goods from the River Usk at Newport to Bristol in the early nineteenth century. It is seen here still in use for sand and gravel supply against the backdrop of the town centre's post-war buildings. The wharf and its paraphernalia have gone and the site is now a car park next to the Riverfront arts centre. During construction work the Newport medieval ship remains were found preserved in the mud nearby. The warehouse has been converted to offices.

Pencil and watercolour on paper, 10 x 22 cm. NPTMG.1992.64
Reproduced with permission of Newport Museum and Art Gallery:

Transporter Bridge, Newport,
1988

Recording the magnificent Newport Transporter Bridge in south Wales became a major task for Falcon in 1988 and resulted in a book on the subject (page 33-4). This sketch emphasises the scale of the pylons and the gondola underneath. The bridge was designed by Robert Haynes and Ferdinand Arnodin and construction began in 1902. It was opened by Viscount Tredegar on 12 September 1906. Although out of commission and under threat at the time Falcon recorded it, the bridge has been restored and is again in regular use. It is recognised as an icon of the city.

Felt pen and watercolour on paper, 21 x 14 cm. NPTMG.1992.71.9 - NPRN 43157
Reproduced with permission of Newport Museum and Art Gallery:

Newport Transporter Bridge, main views, 1988

This image for Falcon's book about the Transporter Bridge provides a view from the east bank of the river and a detailed drawing of the engine house that pulls the gondola across. The stairs to the right of the engine house provide public access to the footbridge across the upper boom: an airy walk!

Pencil, ink and watercolour on paper, 21 x 33 cm.
NPTMG.1992.70.1, NPRN 43157
Reproduced with permission of Newport Museum and Art Gallery:

Newport Transporter Bridge, gondola, 1988

Detail of various components of the gondola, down to the foot control for the turnstiles, the ironwork on the gates and the weathervane on the pilot's house. The gondola, painted in kingfisher blue, carried up to six cars and 120 people who sat on the metal benches under the dagger-board canopies. This bridge has some of the qualities of a ferry boat, as the name 'gondola' implies, and red and white life preservers are needed given that the cold waters of the Usk are all about.

Pencil, ink and watercolour on paper, 21 x 33 cm
NPTMG.1992.70.4, NPRN 43157
Reproduced with permission of Newport Museum and Art Gallery

141

PDH
May '80 S

Industrial Buildings

No type of building has been more threatened by destruction in the last fifty years than the industrial buildings of the nineteenth and twentieth centuries. These were at the heart of the technical, economic and social transformation of Britain during the Industrial Revolution and afterwards. They stood for a narrative with global historical implications, but thousands of textile mills, collieries, steelworks, foundries, flour mills, food factories, breweries and other industrial buildings have been lost as their active life has come to an end.

Protection and adaptive reuse have saved some of the very best industrial buildings, especially the great architect-designed mills and the temples of steam, but many expressions of industrial culture that were more humble, workaday and typical have gone without trace – the patched brickwork of industrial sites altered and altered again to allow for changing needs, the myriad Victorian sheds that housed manufacturing processes, the simply functional mills, the forests of chimneys that once rose above industrial settlements across Britain. It is possible to forget how small were many of the enterprises of the industrial era, such as jam factories on street corners, watchmakers' shops, weaving mills that employed only a few dozen people or coal sales offices that served tightly circumscribed localities. Contrasting with such premises were vast textile factories or giant metal manufacturers like Dowlais ironworks at Merthyr Tydfil, which as early as the 1820s employed 6,000 people and exploited a vast landscape. Little survives now of most of these giant enterprises.

Gone too – even where buildings have been turned to new uses – are the working interiors of industry and their gritty, utilitarian surroundings of cobbled alleys, pipelines, railings or railway sidings. To experience these once characteristic indoor and outdoor environments today you may have to go to industrial museums like Blists Hill or Coalport China Works, or visit some of the few surviving old industrial enterprises. Twenty-first-century industrial sites tend to have very different qualities from those that preceded them – car plants and microprocessor factories are clean, high-tech and isolated from communities. However, Falcon's drawings powerfully project a sense of what industrial buildings of many kinds and sizes in the recent past were all about, how they worked and how people's lives were lived within them and around them.

Coal office, Blaenau Ffestiniog; interior, looking towards counter,
1980

Falcon made two drawings of the interior of the coal office at the railway goods station in Blaenau Ffestiniog, recording the interior with his characteristic eye for detail. Of particular note is the tall wooden counter, a coat hung up on a well-placed nail, and the bundles of papers in bulldog clips and spiked onto a bill-hook dangling from the ceiling. The lamp by the desk is a railway light. The companion drawing detailed the pot-bellied stove that kept the clerk from freezing to death in winter. This coal office was typical of small industrial offices all over Britain. It has since been demolished.

Pencil and watercolour on paper, 21 x 19.5 cm.
FHA 01/081, NPRN 305760

Parc Glynllifon estate gas works, Gwynedd, 1995

Glynllifon was the family seat of the Wynn family, Barons Newborough. The estate model workshops were laid out around two courtyards by the second Baron before 1832, and included stables, cart sheds, a smithy, timber mill, slate mill and a tannery. In this drawing the retort house of the gas works is rendered transparent to show the three retorts and tar filters within; the underground pipe system is also shown. Vignettes show a retort, a gas lamp, a water heater, and the stoker raking out a retort. The site is now in the care of Gwynedd Council.

Print, 30 x 42 cm. FHA 02/51/02 - NPRN 31381

PC's Food and Drink Factory, 1986

Industrial buildings may be discreet parts of the townscape as well as large installations elsewhere. The artist concentrates the viewer's attention on this food factory in Cardiff, reducing the surrounding streets and terraced house to a series of skeletal pencil lines. The terraces have since been demolished and replaced by modern housing and industrial units. The building was a pub, and the 'PC' on its original signage now stands for Poet's Corner.

Pencil and watercolour on paper, 18 x 23 cm. FHA 02/47 - NPRN 301223

Spillers' curved warehouse, Cardiff, 1987

This is one of a series of preparatory drawings made in 1987 for an exhibition at the Andrew Knight Gallery in Cardiff. Nearly all the finished drawings were sold; their whereabouts are now unknown. The warehouse was built in 1893 as part of a complex of steam roller flour mills processing 100,000 tons of wheat a year. The unusual north face was curved to follow the line of a railway siding. The warehouse has now been converted into apartments.

Pencil on paper, *top, left:* 42 x 74 cm. FHA 02/59, *top right:* 27 x 17.5 cm. FHA 11/02/02 and *above:* 25 x 14 cm. FHA 11/86/02 - NPRN 301223

Welsh Brewers Cardiff, 1987

Another of the artist's preparatory drawings for his 1987 Cardiff exhibition sets out the preparations for a study that was never completed of one of the Cardiff breweries, rising above an abruptly terminated street. Note the lines controlling perspective and the circles emphasising the circular towers, the lightly-drawn telephone wires and the steam rising from the left tower. A solitary figure provides a sense of scale.

Pencil on paper, 39 x 35 cm. FHA 02/60 - NPRN 301223

Dowlais stables, 1987

The drawing exudes outrage at the neglect and destruction of Merthyr's industrial heritage, and is an example of the quick sketches the artist makes when travelling. The long, low building with the raised gatehouse is Dowlais Ironworks stables, which were built for Sir Josiah John Guest in 1820. They fell out of use in the 1930s and became derelict. In the late 1970s unauthorised demolition was started. It was halted but the buildings remained roofless for several years. They have since been rebuilt as flats. Standing amid the largely cleared site of the ironworks in the foreground is the 1909 blowing engine house, now part of a chocolate factory. These are the only surviving structures of what was once the world's largest ironworks.

Felt pen, watercolour and pencil on paper, 11 x 18 cm.
FHA 02/76, NPRN 34085

Hydraulic power house chimney, Newcastle upon Tyne, 1979

One of Falcon's two detailed architectural illustrations of ornate chimneys, drawn as true elevations without perspective; chimneys and other tall buildings cannot otherwise be viewed in this way. Hydraulic power, transmitted through pipes by water under pressure, was pioneered in Newcastle by Sir William Armstrong. At first, the domestic water supply pressure was used to provide power, but when this became inadequate steam pumping stations were built, with the water pressurised under weighted cylinders. Tens of thousands of chimneys across Britain vented the fires that raised the steam that ran the engines that powered industry in the nineteenth century. Very few survive.

Finished gelatine print and watercolour on paper, 67 x 14 cm.
FHA 03/02

Disused factory at night, Meadow Street, Coventry, 1975

Falcon began drawing buildings whilst he was at Coventry School of Art in the 1950s, and he returned time and time again to search out and record the city as its old buildings were destroyed in post-war redevelopment. In the nineteenth century, Coventry's two major industries were silk ribbon weaving and watch-making, and this derelict factory with its long upper window may have housed one or the other. The artist's choice of a night view, with a single street lamp illuminating the frontage, emphasises the sense of decay.

Ink and chalk on paper, 11 x 15 cm. FHA 03/08

Gas House Tunnel, Grimsby,
1973

This drawing captures a memory of Falcon's birth town, Grimsby, where he remembered the gas works and the railways, and the incessant noise of shunting locomotives close to the family home. The tall retort building of the gas works stands beyond the railway, under which runs a low, dark pedestrian tunnel. The figure emphasises the scale of the tunnel but also hints at a story remembered by the artist about a murder committed there.

Chalk and crayon on paper, 20 x 18 cm. FHA 03/12

Rotherham and Son, Spon End, Coventry, 1976

The drawing was probably made during one of Falcon's short visits to Coventry from his London bed-sit. He had become painfully aware of the speed at which the Coventry of his childhood was disappearing before the onslaught of new development. Premises such as these for a single, small business were as much at risk as those of larger industries on the decline. The drawing emphasises the heavy stone arch head and lintels, the ornamental door casing and the name board with its stylish lettering, whilst the brick walls are represented only by shading. Falcon suspected that the house, with its workshop wing at the back, had once belonged to a master watchmaker.

Pencil on tracing paper, 23 x 16 cm. FHA 03/27

Isaac Lord, Ipswich, 1973

The drawing shows part of a complex of commercial buildings, as seen from Ipswich's quayside, which had developed at the rear of a fifteenth-century merchant's house. The brick gable is the end of a very long building, part of which was a warehouse and showroom where woollen cloth was collected from Suffolk's domestic weavers, prior to export. Semi-vernacular buildings in waterside locations have been easier to put to new use than many other industrial buildings. This and the malting kiln have now become a waterside pub.

Pencil and water colour on paper, 15 x 7 cm. FHA 03/48

Blackdown Mill, Warwickshire, 1966

This water-powered corn mill near Leamington Spa was built in two periods; the left-hand end in the eighteenth century and the near end, with a weatherboarded upper storey, in the nineteenth. The curved wall and decorative balconies may be tokens of a desire to beautify an industrial building. The waterwheel was in the centre, under the arched opening, which bridges the underground tailrace. The mill is now a private house but the hoist in the projecting gable and the tall chimney behind the mill are among the features that survive. This is among Falcon's earliest surviving drawings of industrial buildings, and its dark mood and strange light recall the contemporary work of the illustrator Alan Sorrell.

Ink on paper, 10.5 x 16 cm.   FHA 03/56

Weaver's house and workshop, Coventry, 1975

The weaving of silk ribbons was established in several Midlands towns, but by the 1820s Coventry had become dominant, protected by prohibition and later by tariffs on imported goods. Many weavers had their looms in workshops on the upper storey. This was clearly more than a single-family enterprise like most domestic industries, having a large house at the far end but an extensive areas of well-lit workshops and a store, and showing signs of frequent alteration and expansion. Despite its title, it is not certain whether this was originally a weaver's or a watchmaker's workshop; both would be built to maximise the light falling on the looms or benches. He drew it to show the house occupied; all the original buildings in Meadow Street have been demolished.

Gelatine print and watercolour on paper, 8.5 x 19.5 cm. FHA 03/60

Rudge Street, Coventry, 1975

This drawing shows a terrace of houses Falcon observed in 1967 and drew up in 1975. They were asymmetrical, with three-storeys at the rear but two storeys at the front, a type favoured by watchmakers who would work at benches under the long windows on the top floor. This row was demolished in the 1960s to make way for the Coventry ring road.

Chalk and ink on paper, 6.5 x 8.5 cm. FHA 03/79

Eli Green's Cottage Factory, Coventry: coal being delivered, 1977

Coventry's silk ribbon weavers resisted the establishment of factories, even burning down the earliest ones. Cottage factories provided an alternative, whereby rows of houses with 'top shops' for working were rented out to independent weavers who paid fees for power from a common steam engine. Eli Green's factory was built in 1858-59 (see also pages 37-8). Falcon made many sketches during the demolition of the buildings and later developed a series of finished reconstructions of the factory at its height. In this image, a carter is delivering coal to fuel the steam boilers in the engine house that was at the centre of the complex in the early morning. Lights burn behind the large windows of the top-shops, to which power from the engine was taken by line shafting.

Chalk and ink on paper, 11 x 9.5 cm. FHA 03/82

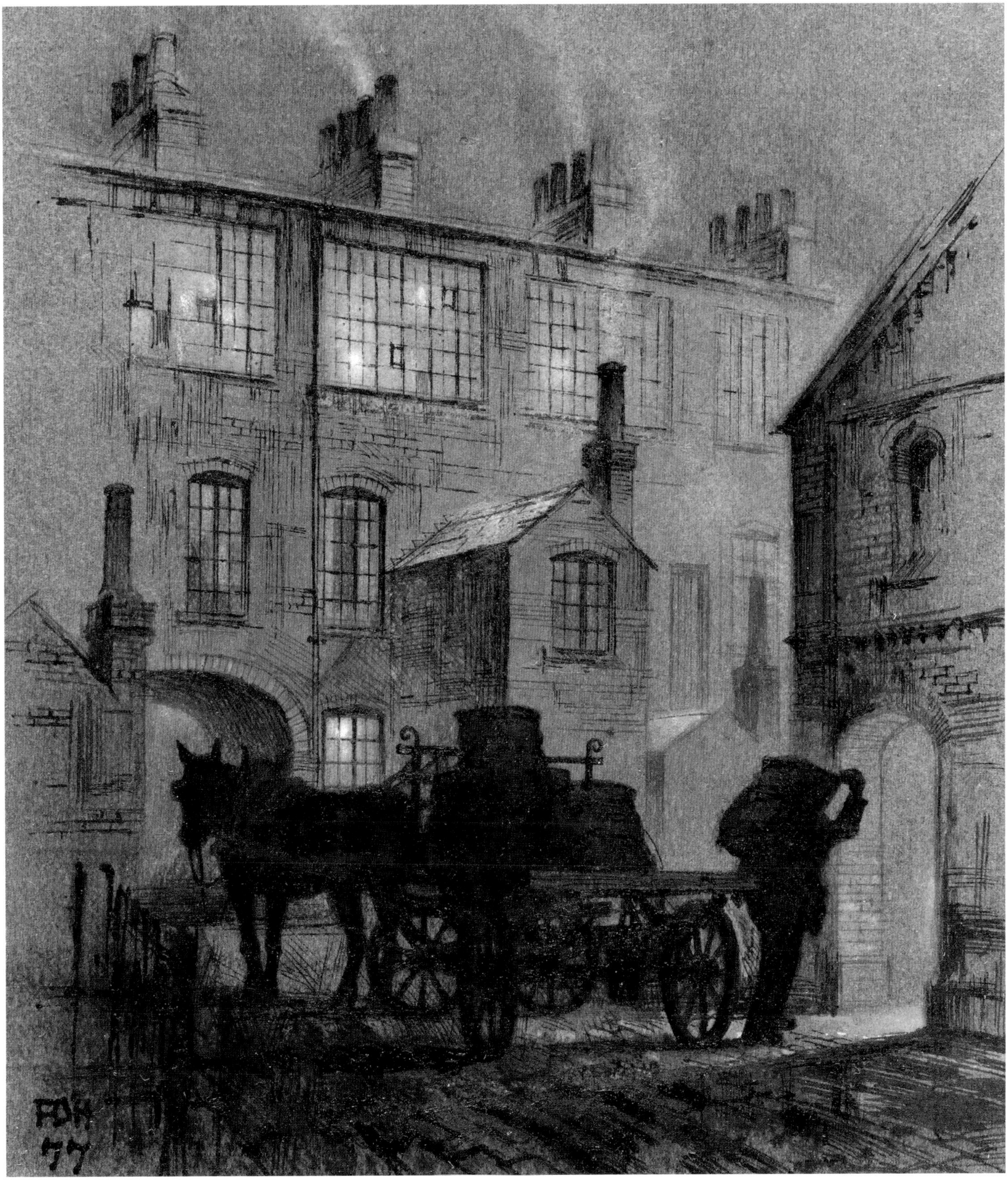
FDH
77

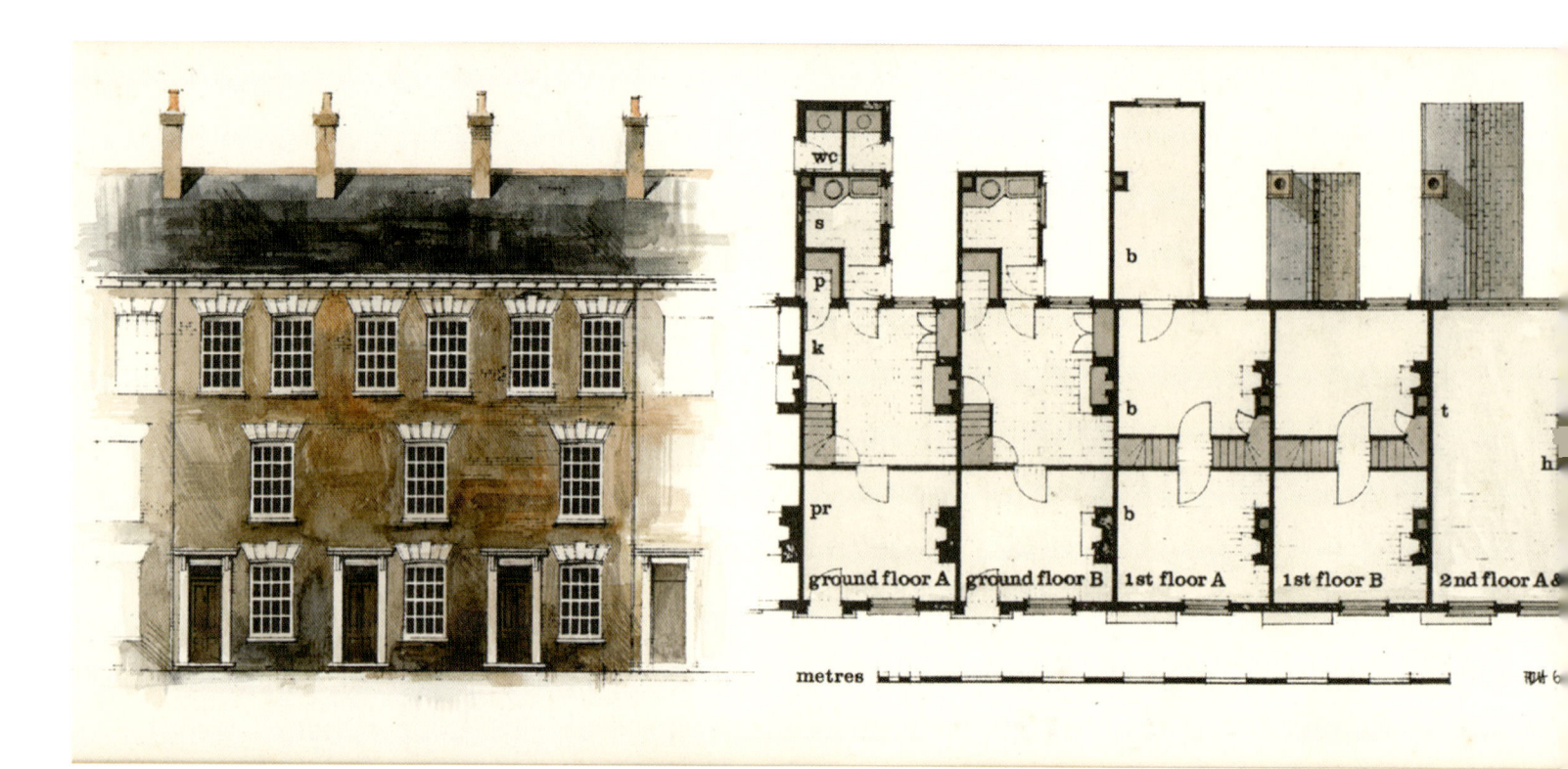

Eli Green's Cottage Factory, Coventry: gardening, 1977

An idealised reconstruction of life in the cottage factory, with the weaver and his family tending the gardens in the courtyard within the triangle. A woman nurses her child. Overhead the line shaft carrying power to the lofts crosses between the rows. In this series of drawings, Falcon was sometimes at a loss to decide whether he ought to record the reality of the site at the end of its life or to reconstruct its working years, in good times or in bad; here the factory appears to prosper.

Chalk and ink on sepia paper, 11 x 9.5 cm FHA 03/83

s scullery
p pantry
k kitchen: living room
pr parlour
b bedroom
t topshop: weaving rm
h hatch
ss steam shaft

Eli Green's Cottage Factory, Coventry: plan, elevation and section, 1977

Falcon's site sketches have been developed into a comprehensive record of this fascinating industrial enterprise. Here we are presented with scale drawings of the front and rear elevations, a section (showing that the houses were well appointed, with fireplaces in four of the five domestic rooms), and a ground plan. Each house had its own toilet, which were built in pairs at the end of alternate rear extensions. Note the very tall upper storey, with sufficient height for accommodating the Jacquard looms, and the extra windows to light the delicate work.

Pencil, ink and letraset on paper, 28 x 88 cm. FHA 03/85

Eli Green's Cottage Factory, Coventry: top shop with loom, 1979

Jacquard looms were invented in 1801 and introduced into Coventry in 1823; by 1841 there were more than two thousand in the city. They automated the process of making intricate patterns, using sets of punched cards to control the warp threads, often hundreds of cards to a set. The drawing shows a Jacquard loom in a top shop, with the work illuminated by the large window and the Jacquard mounted above the loom, in the apex of the roof. Access into the topshop was by steep stairs with a trap door through the floor.

Pencil on paper, 11 x 10 cm. FHA 03/87

Cottage Factory at Hillfields, Coventry

Built in 1858-9 by Eli Green, master manufacturer of ribbons, to accommodate sixty six weavers and their families. Each dwelling had its own topshop where the family worked the looms. Power was provided by a central steam engine, and transmitted to the topshops by means of shafting which ran round the entire factory at roof level. The factory, known locally as Eli Green's Triangle, was demolished in 1969-70.   FDH 69/70

Eli Green's Cottage Factory, Coventry: weaver's view, 1976

The artist has produced a reconstruction, from his many site sketches, of the view from the back window at the end of one terrace over the triangular courtyard to the two other terraces. Washing flutters on the line, smoke rises from the chimneys and the central engine house, and everything seems in order. However the silk ribbon industry collapsed in 1860, only a year after the completion of Eli Green's Cottage Factory.

Chalk and ink on paper, 16 x 38 cm. FHA 03/83

Eli Green's Cottage Factory, Coventry, 1976

The cottage factories planned in the 1850s with rows of houses linked to a common power source enabled the weavers to remain their own masters. Eli Green's factory consisted of 67 cottages in three terraces, enclosing a triangular courtyard. In the widest part of the court was an engine and boiler house, and power was transmitted by rotating shafts to and along each row to the loom-shops on the top floor. The shaft can be seen on the right between two terraces. Weavers and their families rented the cottages and paid a fee for power to drive their loom.

Ink on tracing paper, 19 x 43 cm. FHA 03/86

Yellow lorry emerging from Ticklers, Grimsby, 1979

This represents one of Falcon's earliest memories of his home town, made into a finished drawing forty years after the image fixed itself in his consciousness. Tickler's Preserves was at the back of his house. Rain has turned the cobbled street into a mirror reflecting the brightly coloured lorry and the people. But he was dissatisfied with his drawing of the handcart, and scribbled over it.

Pencil and water colour on paper, 20 x 15 cm. FHA 03/25

Uskside Ironworks, Newport, 1987

Many industrial buildings show the evidence of their frequent alteration over time. Uskside Ironworks, a large foundry on Church Street in Newport's Pillgwenlly district, had irregular buildings separated by a street, but the company managed to get permission to build gates at each end and convert the street into a yard. The drawing shows one of the gates, but Falcon was fascinated by the way in which huge corrugated iron sheds had been erected over the old buildings and the former street, totally ignoring their former plan. The buildings are still in light industrial use.

Pencil and watercolour on paper, 30 x 63 cm. NPTMG.1992.45
Reproduced with permission of Newport Museum and Art Gallery:

Mill Town, Lydgate, Lancashire, 1978

Lancashire drawings are rare in Falcon's collection, and as there are several Lydgates in Lancashire, this one has not yet been identified with certainty. Nonetheless, it exudes the atmosphere of a north Lancashire mill town: the stone-built terraced housing, the retaining wall blackened with soot, the multi-storey mill looming over the houses, and the smoking chimneys adding their quota to the leaden grey, rain-filled sky.

Pencil on paper, 9.5 x 18 cm. FHA 03/913

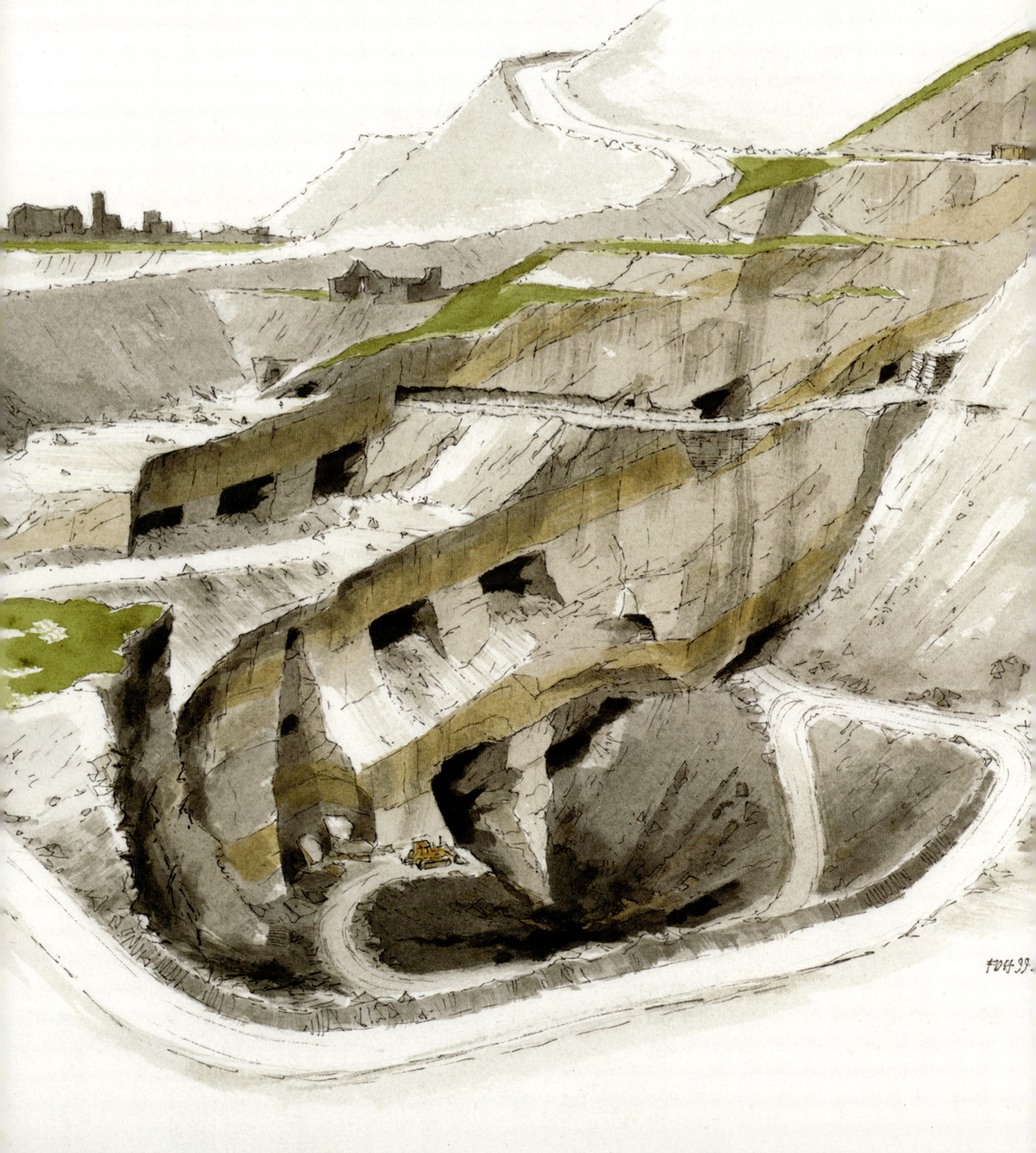

The Landscape of Slate

The Welsh slate industry is renowned for the quality of its products, especially its roofing slates and slabs. In its heyday during the late nineteenth century and shortly afterwards, slates were exported from the main production areas in Caernarfonshire and Merioneth to markets all over the world. The industry affected the visual character of numerous British 'worktowns', providing the default roofing material for mill settlements in Lancashire and Yorkshire, mining villages in the south Wales valleys, housing across London and many other townscapes, as well as providing for individual buildings all over the world. Slate also created its own worktowns in the producing areas – places such as Bethesda, Penygroes, Deiniolen and Nantlle where towns and villages built of slate were surrounded by whole landscapes dedicated to the quarrying, mining, processing and transport of the material. The culture and technology of the north Wales slate industry, as well as its products, were influential around the world, and its outstanding landscapes may become a World Heritage Site.

Falcon's exploration of the industry has focused on Blaenau Ffestiniog, the largest of the slate towns and one of the greatest producing areas, with remains of twenty quarries. He began documenting it in the late 1960s and has continued ever since, in particular energised by a commission in 1996 from the Snowdonia Society. Blaenau Ffestiniog's buildings appear in all sections of this book.

Part of the fascination of the slate quarrying landscape is that the vastness of the industry's impact – digging hundreds of feet into mountainsides and spreading tips over vast tracts of land – combines with the human scale and intricate design of so many of its features. Falcon points out that this is because they were created before the days of earth-moving machines and mechanised processing equipment. He says, 'Every piece of slate that makes up the huge waste tips was moved by hand [...] with intelligence and economy of effort.' This is indeed a hand-made landscape, of quarries and waste tips, dams and watercourses, tramways, drum-houses and inclines, mills and workshops, housing and offices, 'each with its own distinctive purpose and rugged beauty, and each fitted to its location with a tidy compactness and logic that is totally satisfying.'[15]

The form of extraction varied across the slate producing areas, from underground mining around Blaenau and Corris to deep pits in the Nantlle valley and hillside quarries at Llanberis and Penrhyn. But many of the qualities seen at Blaenau are common to slate-producing landscapes everywhere. Above all, each of these areas expresses the sublime and awe-inspiring power of both the natural geology that produces slate and the human agency that attempts to master it. The vertiginous scale of the quarry landscapes and the perilousness of being within them are hard to express in two-dimensional imagery. Falcon suggests that such subjects defy recording; he argues that they have to be experienced, and so have to be preserved.

Exposed chambers - Foty and Bowydd quarry, 1977 (detail)

At Blaenau Ffestiniog slate was mined in large underground chambers following the steeply dipping slate beds, leaving pillars of rock to hold up the roof. These chambers have been almost totally obscured by modern working, but here the top has been taken off, revealing the subterranean tunnels and chambers, including one tunnel sliced through laterally to appear as though in a drawn section. To the left are the ruins of Maenofferen Cottages and Quarrybank House (in the trees), which once accommodated workers and the manager of Maenofferen quarries. The stone pillar was one of a line that once supported wooden troughs bringing water to one of the slate mills, which were powered by waterwheels.

Pencil, ink and watercolour on paper, 29 x 47 cm.
FHA 01/42 - NPRN 415760

The Oakeley Gash, 1974

A panorama of the terraced working of the Oakeley slate quarries, seen as one enters Blaenau Ffestiniog from the north over the Crimea pass. To the left are the terraced houses of Tal-y-Waenydd, and beyond them are the Llechwedd quarries and slate mill. Small vignettes provide a plan and section of the Oakeley workings, which extended from an altitude of 1,200 feet to below sea level. Above, the Oakeley 'pit' underground levels are set against a profile of the mountains, with roads, tracks and tramways indicated in orange.

Pencil, ink and watercolour on paper, 24 x 80 cm.
FHA 01/08/02 - NPRN 404307

Blaenau Ffestiniog from Pengwndwn, 1999

The drawing is typical of several panoramas in which the artist expresses his concern to show Blaenau Ffestiniog in harmony with the landscape. This view from the south towards the head of the Vale of Ffestiniog emphasises the ring of mountains and the dark tips of slate waste that surround and dominate the town, which has been Falcon's home since 1968. His mill home is above the terraced houses on the right of the drawing, to the left of the waterfall.

Pencil, ink and watercolour on paper, 17 x 103 cm. FHA FHA 01/003 - NPRN 305760

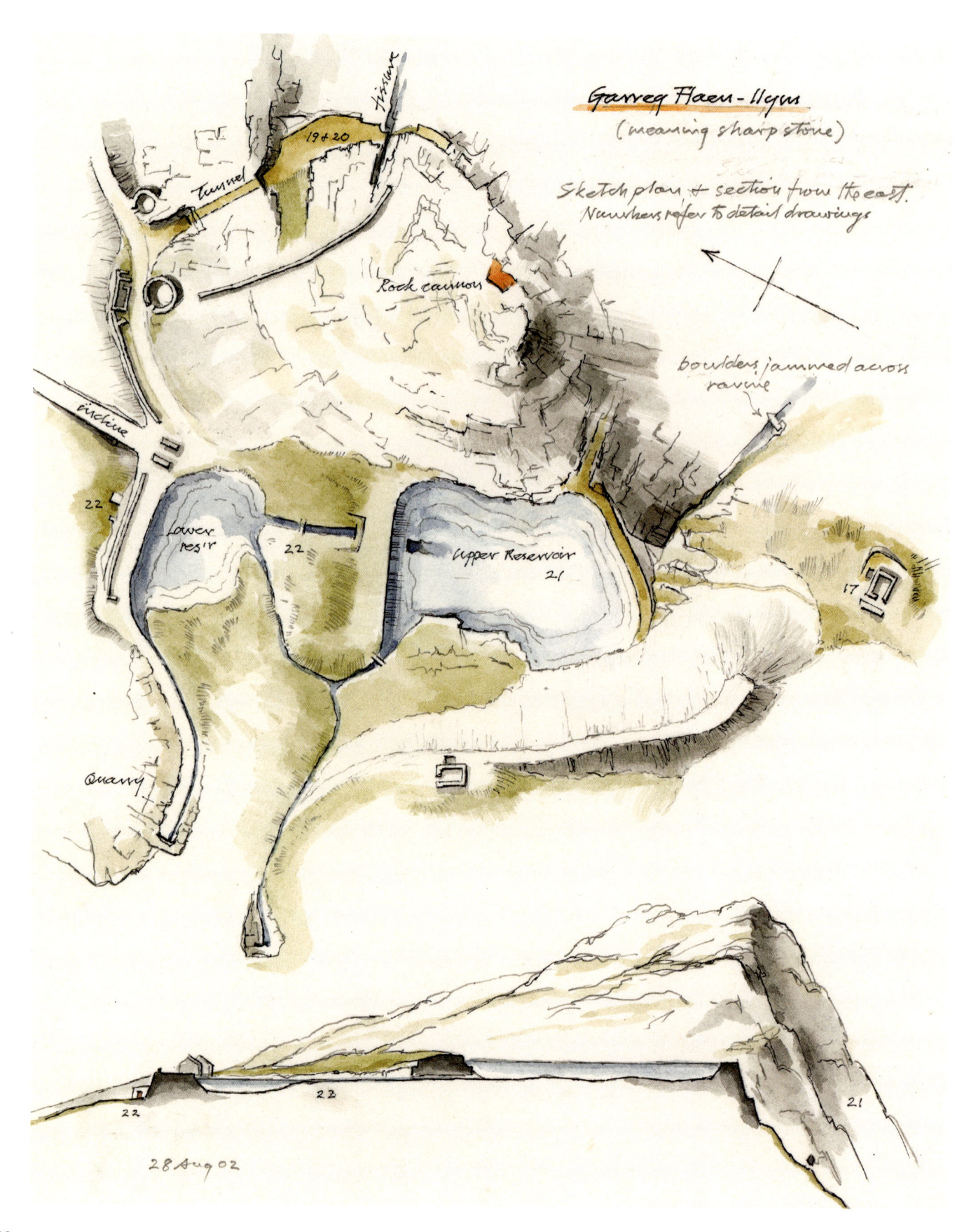

Garreg Flaen-llyn
(meaning sharp stone)

Sketch plan & section from the east.
Numbers refer to detail drawings

boulders jammed across ravine

Tunnel — Fissure — 19 & 20
Rock cannon
incline
22 — Lower res'r — 22 — Upper Reservoir 21
Quarry
17

22 — 22 — 21

28 Aug 02

168

Garreg Flaen-llym and the reservoirs,
detail plan and section drawing of top dam, 2002

Garreg Flaen-llym is the prominent rock that towers over Blaenau Ffestiniog on the west side. The two reservoirs, impounded by stone-faced dams on this challenging site, supplied water to slate mills on the upper levels of the Oakeley quarries. The plan records various small buildings and other elements of this remote landscape of quarrying. At the summit of the mountain can be found the remains of a rock cannon, a form of traditional celebration whereby a series of holes were drilled in the rock, filled with gunpowder and fired in sequence to produce a rhythm or tune.

Pencil, ink and watercolour on paper, 30 x 42 cm
FHA 01/43 - NPRN 404307.

Tan-y-grisiau Terrace, 1987

This is a terrace of eleven houses standing on a rocky shelf above the eponymous straggling village to the south west of Blaenau Ffestiniog, beneath the steep slopes of Graig Nyth-y-Gigfran. Many individual houses and short terraces were found sites in this craggy terrain, sometimes fitted inventively round the overhanging rocks. Here the builder provided a morsel of architectural style and symmetry by adding a gable to the middle house.

Pencil, ink and watercolour on paper, 20 x 32 cm.
FHA 01/54 - NPRN 416028

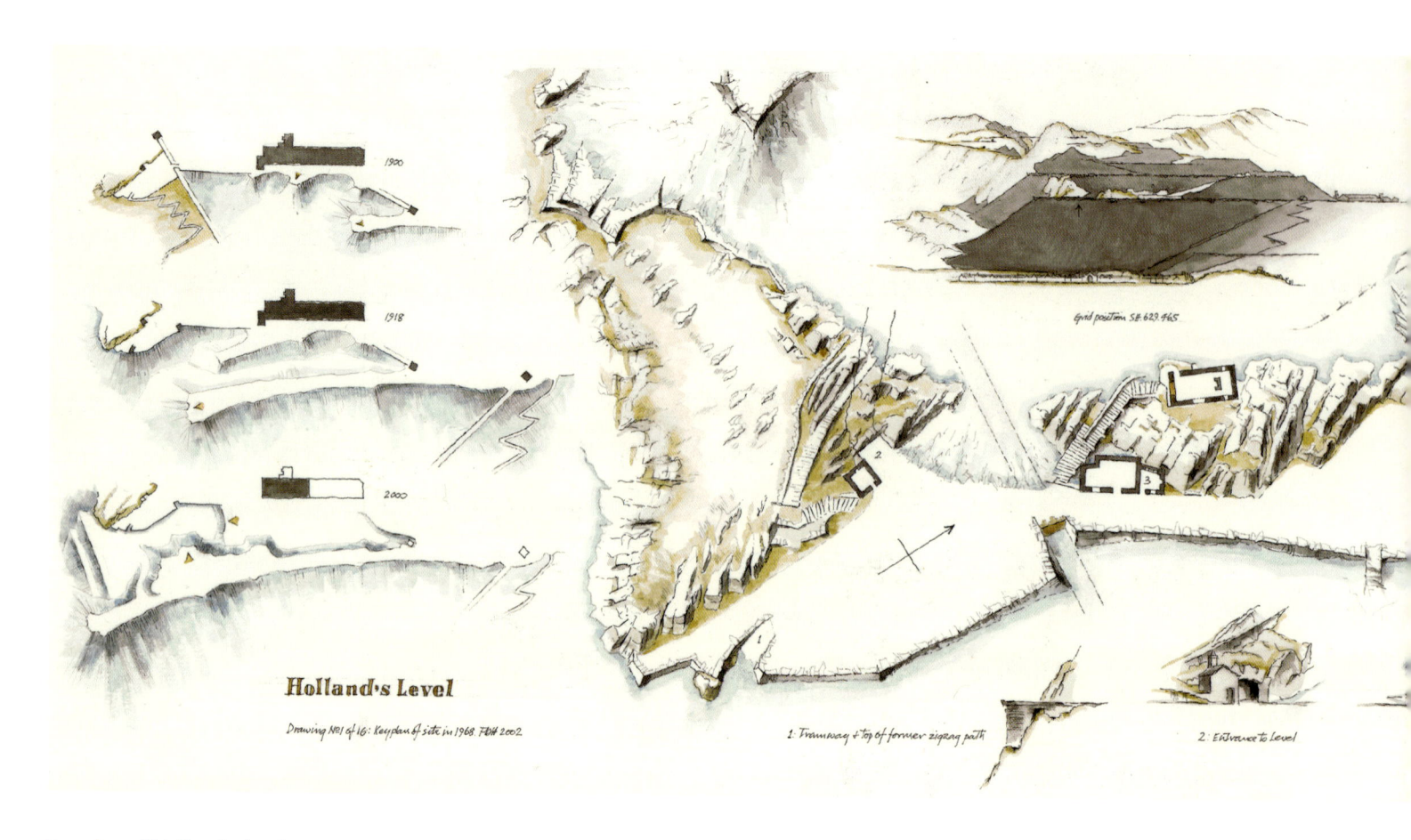

Key plan of Holland's level, 2002

The drawing combines a general plan of the Holland's level with vignettes of the buildings, tramways and inclines, many of which Falcon has illustrated in greater detail elsewhere. On the left are three miniature plans showing the extent of the slate mill and tipping at different dates in the quarry's development. Although the preliminary records were made in 1968, the finished drawing was completed in 2002.

Pencil, ink and watercolour on paper, 27 x 103 cm.
FHA 01/006 - NPRN 415776

Holland's level - aerial view of house by cutting, chimney and incline, 2001

Here the artist records some of the features of Holland's level slate quarry as he saw them in 1968 – a cottage, part of the slate mill and a tramway cutting – as seen from normal eye level. But then he adopts a bird's eye view so as to emphasise the relationships between the features. Quarrying here began in 1827 and the steam-powered slate mill was built in about 1860. All is now derelict, the chimney has gone and the features are under threat from tipping and the ravages of the weather.

Pencil, ink and watercolour on paper, 22 x 41 cm.
FHA 01/072 - NPRN 415776

circular building 150 m

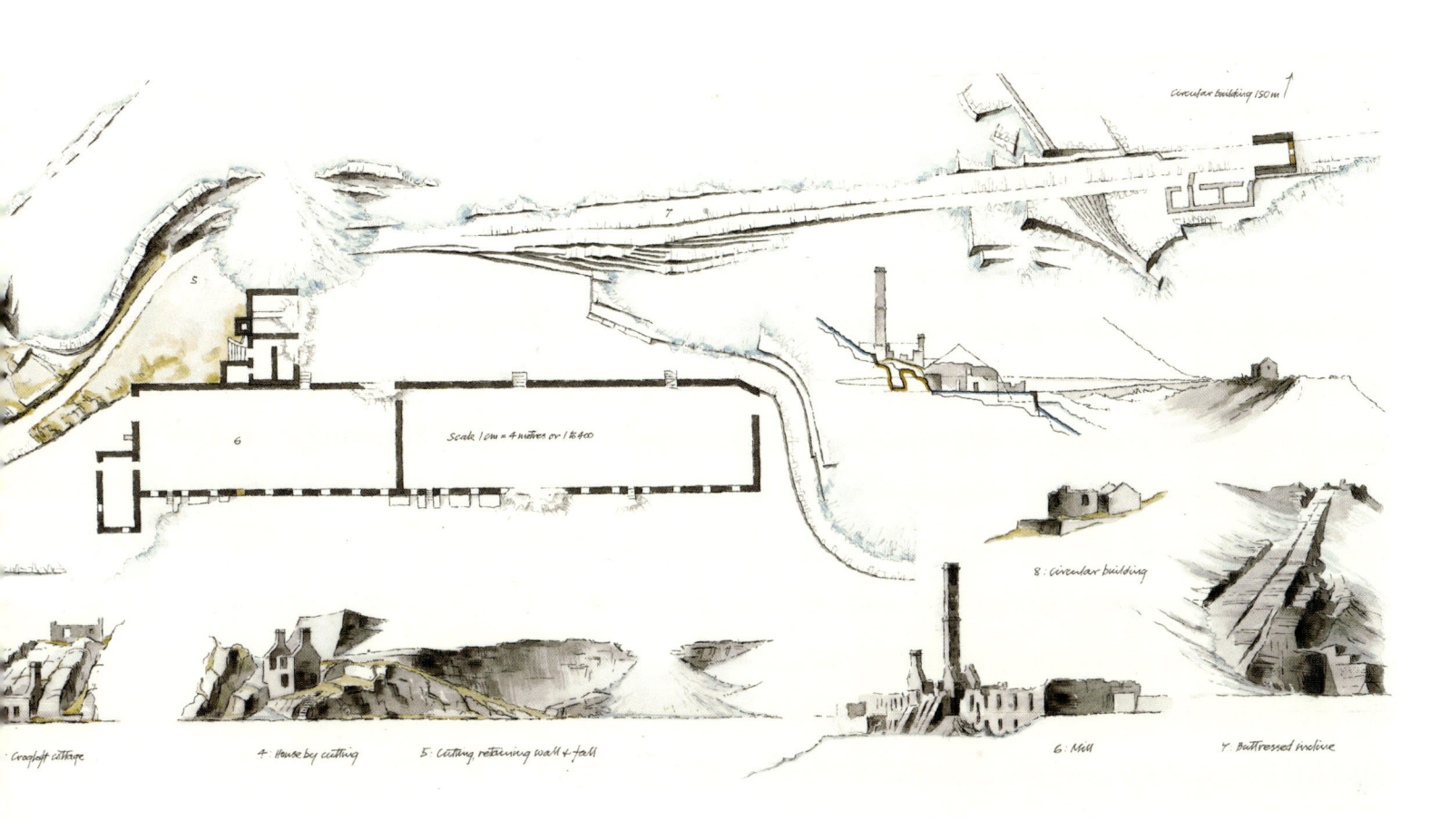

Scale 1 cm = 4 metres or 1 to 400

8: Circular building

3: Craglleft cottage   4: House by cutting   5: Cutting retaining wall & fall   6: Mill   7: Buttressed incline

Holland's Level:
Cutting, Retaining Walls
& Slate Falls

Holland's level - buttressed incline, 2001

In these four views of the lines of a former incline and a flight of steps, the artist concentrates on the textures of the slopes of waste slate and the dry-stone methods used in construction. Different shades of grey bring out the shadows and give depth to the drawing. These are relict features in a state of ruin, and the buttresses under the incline speak of the problems of building and maintaining it in such a difficult landscape.

Pencil, ink and watercolour on paper, 30 x 38 cm.
FHA 01/074 - NPRN 415776

Holland's level - mill looking towards Garreg Flaen-llyn, 2002

Holland's quarry was established in 1827 and the steam-powered slate mill was built on Holland's level in about 1860. Finished slates were lowered down an incline to the Ffestiniog Railway. In 1878, Holland's became part of the Oakeley quarries. This level has been widened by modern tipping which still continues; the chimney has collapsed and the nearer (north) half of the mill has been demolished. This is one of several drawings which document the site in detail as it was in 1967, when Falcon and his friend Rita first saw it. It was still virtually the same in 2002. This is one of Falcon's own favourite drawings.

Pencil, ink and watercolour on paper, 16 x 29 cm.
FHA 01/077 - NPRN 415776

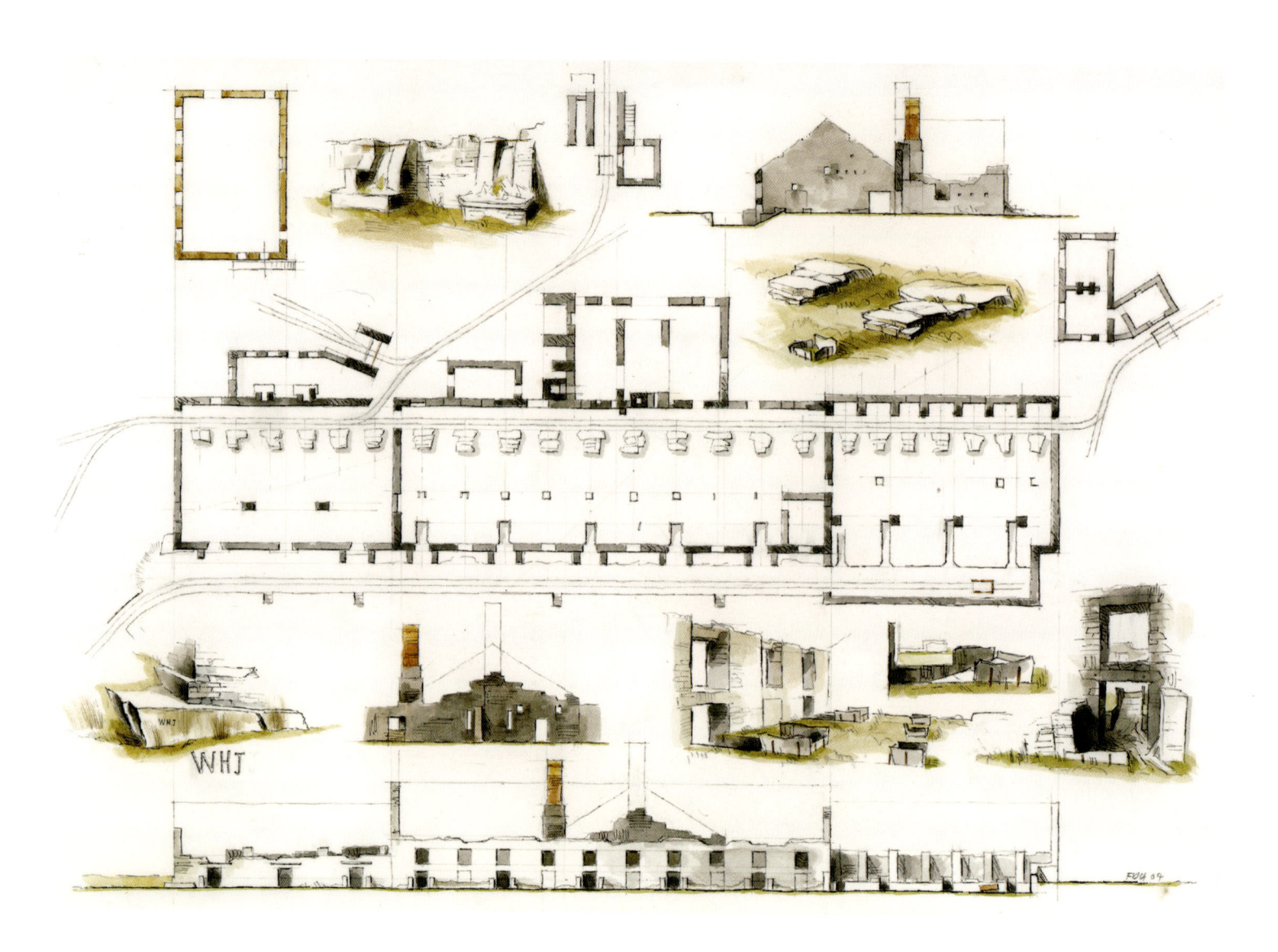

Steam Mill, Diffwys quarry, drawing, plan and elevations, 2004

High above the east side of Blaenau Ffestiniog, the ruins of Diffwys steam mill still dominate the skyline. This drawing forms an accurate archaeological record showing the tramways which brought slate blocks into the mill to be sawn on twenty-three slate saws then passed to the trimmers on the south side, where there was a truck to carry away the waste. The steam engine and boiler were in the extension on the north side. There was also a smithy. The heads of two inclines can be seen. Initials carved on the foundation block are also recorded. This mill superseded Melin Pant-yr-ynn and the oblong plan at top left shows this earlier mill for comparative scale.

Pencil, ink and watercolour on paper, 31 x 42 cm
FHA 01/093, NPRN 415671

Overhanging rock, High Street, 1987

Blaenau Ffestiniog is hemmed in by steep rocky cliffs and towering mountains of slate waste, and this rocky overhang dramatically punctuates the urban landscape along the main road in the town. Beyond, accessed by the narrow lane that climbs under the overhang, are the late nineteenth-century terrace houses of Summerhill.

Pencil and watercolour on paper, 19 x 18 cm
FHA 01/119, NPRN 417371

175

Remains of Bonc Goedai winding house, Oakeley quarry, 1998

By the time this drawing was made, one side of the winding house had been demolished to make way for a new road, and the frame that supported the drum had been sawn through, leaving circular marks on the jutting timbers where the drum had revolved. The artist's technique emphasises the mixture of large, sawn slate slabs and smaller infill pieces in the walls. The incline was one of a series raising blocks of slate from the underground galleries, and the building housed the electric winding mechanism.

Ink and watercolour on paper, 16 x 29 cm. FHA 01/125 - NPRN 417171

Two views of Pant-yr-ynn slate mill, 2007

Pant-yr-ynn mill was in use in 1846 by the Diffwys Casson quarry, on a site where their cart road crossed a stream which could provide power. It was replaced by steam-powered mills from the 1860s, and became a school. Then in 1881 it was converted into a woollen mill by Jacob Jones & Son and worked until 1964, when it was closed down and the machinery scrapped. The original part of the building is preserved with its overhead line-shafting, and the 24-feet diameter overshot waterwheel has been restored to working order. It is now Falcon's home and gallery (see pages 22-28).

Pencil and watercolour on paper, 30 x 21 cm. FHA 01/128 - NPRN 28620

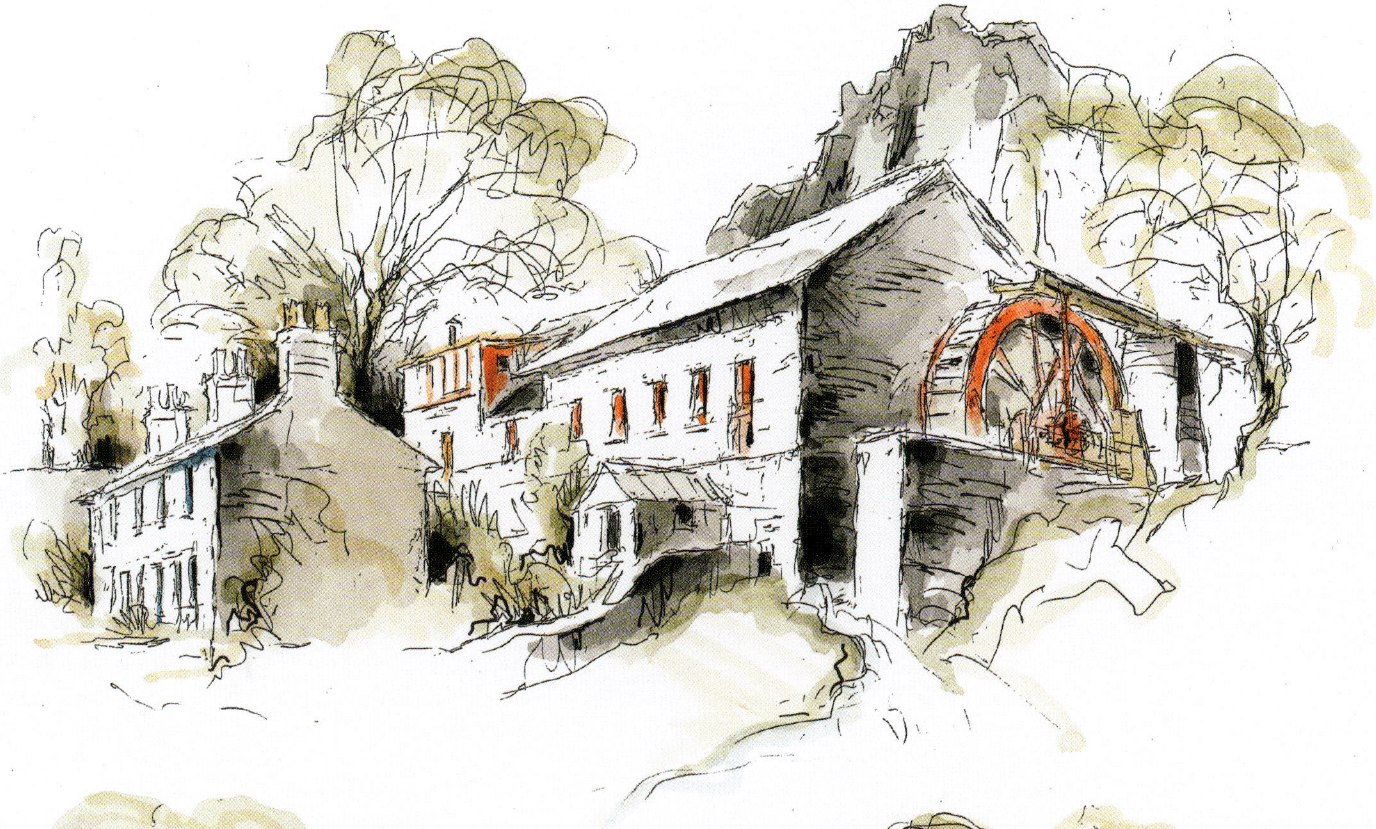

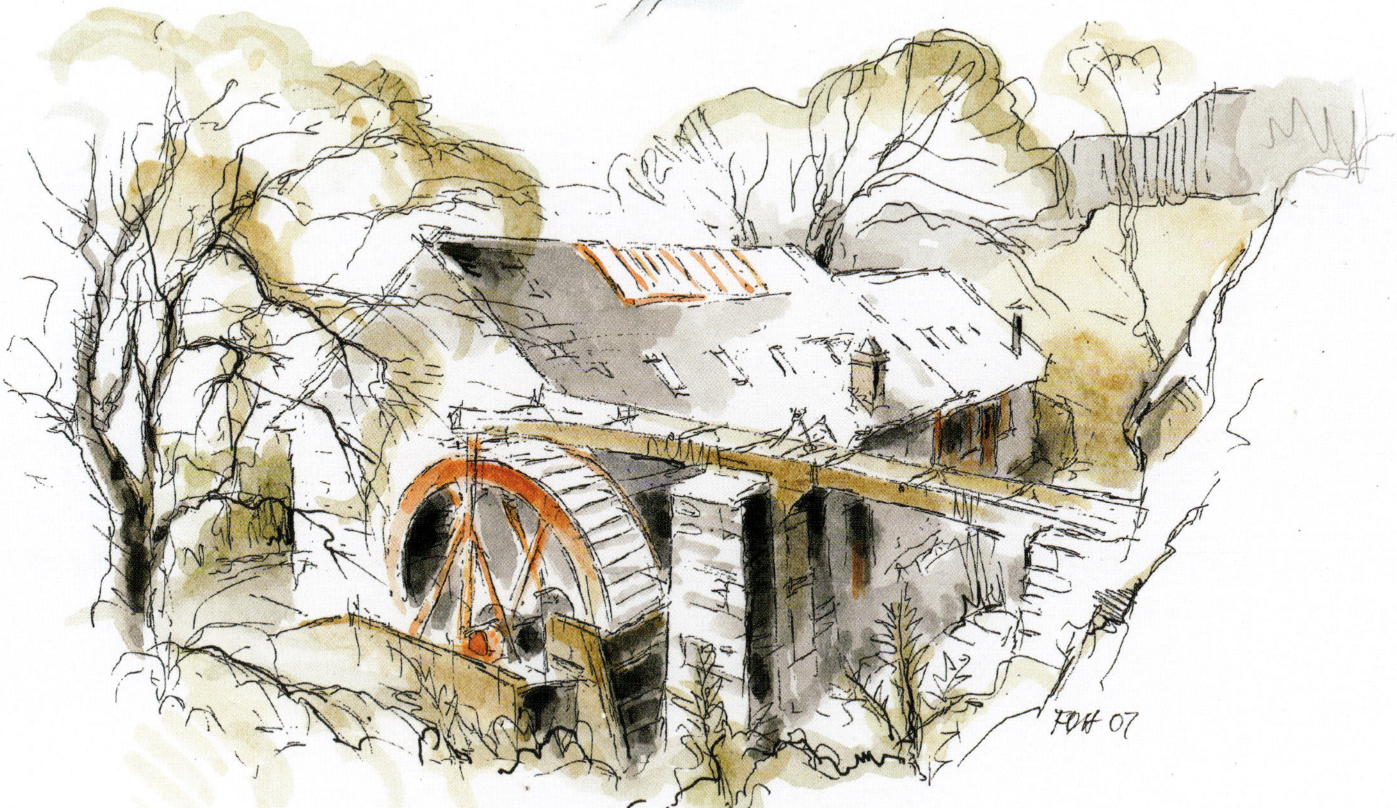
FOH 07

Rhosydd drum house to Croesor incline, 2003

This drawing captures the extraordinary synergy in the slate quarrying landscape between the natural rock and man-made slate structures. However, the artist himself says it is not possible to capture the cliff-edge vertigo of such a location, let alone the feeling of building such structures in it. Rhosydd quarry sent its slates to Porthmadog on the horse-drawn Croesor tramway, and its own tramway passed across the precipitous head of Cwm Croesor to the head of the steepest quarry incline in Wales. Built in 1864, the incline was designed with a catenary profile by Charles Spooner, and fell 205 metres; the steepest part at the top had a gradient of 46 degrees. The site was so restricted that the rope drum had to be placed 17 metres above the incline brow, with the brakes controlled by cables and a ship's wheel fastened to the large horizontal slab.

Pencil, ink and watercolour on paper, 30 x 42 cm.
FHA 01/175/03, NPRN 400884

Rhiwbach tramway crossing Llyn Bowydd dam, 2008

The Rhiwbach tramway connected several quarries on the north side of Manod Mawr and at the head of Cwm Penmachno to the Ffestiniog railway. Here the tramway crossed the stone-banked dam that impounded Llyn Bowydd, a reservoir for the slate quarries. The line is gently graded to allow wagons to move by gravity as far as the counterbalance drum house that can be seen in the distance, at the head of the first of three inclines leading down to Blaenau Ffestiniog.

Pencil, ink and watercolour on paper, 13 x 28 cm.
FHA 01/172 - NPRN 65714

Maenofferen quarry - winding house, detail drawing, 1999

Falcon has made a series of detailed drawings of Maenofferen quarry. A panorama is on page 44 and the following pages show individual features. This drawing records the winding house at the head of the incline from the underground galleries. Blocks of slate were hauled up by electric motors, their speed controlled by iron plates lowered into barrels of sulphuric acid. The windows provided a view down the incline, and the brake lever raised a stop, which prevented wagons running away by gravity. Beyond is the unhooker's cabin, its wall cut away to allow large blocks to pass.

Pencil, ink and watercolour on paper, 20 x 20 cm. FHA 01/061 - NPRN 416518

Maenofferen quarry - winding house, detail drawing from chimney side, 1999

The drawing records the winding house and unhooker's cabin at the head of the Maenofferen incline, with the incline itself disappearing into the bowels of the earth beyond. On the left are a chimney stack and its cranked flue, remaining from the time when the incline was powered by a steam engine.

Pencil, ink and watercolour on paper, 16 x 25 cm. FHA 01/062 - NPRN 416518

Maenofferen quarry - looking to exit tunnel from beneath winding house, 1999

At Maenofferen, slate was worked in underground chambers and raised to the surface by an electrically-powered incline. This detail shows the office for the 'unhooker', who attached and detached wagons from the ropes at the head of the incline. To the right the tramway disappears into a short tunnel which led to the slate mill, where blocks were sawn to size and split into slates.

Pencil, ink and watercolour on paper, 16 x 21 cm.
FHA 01/179 - NPRN 415947 and NPRN 415934

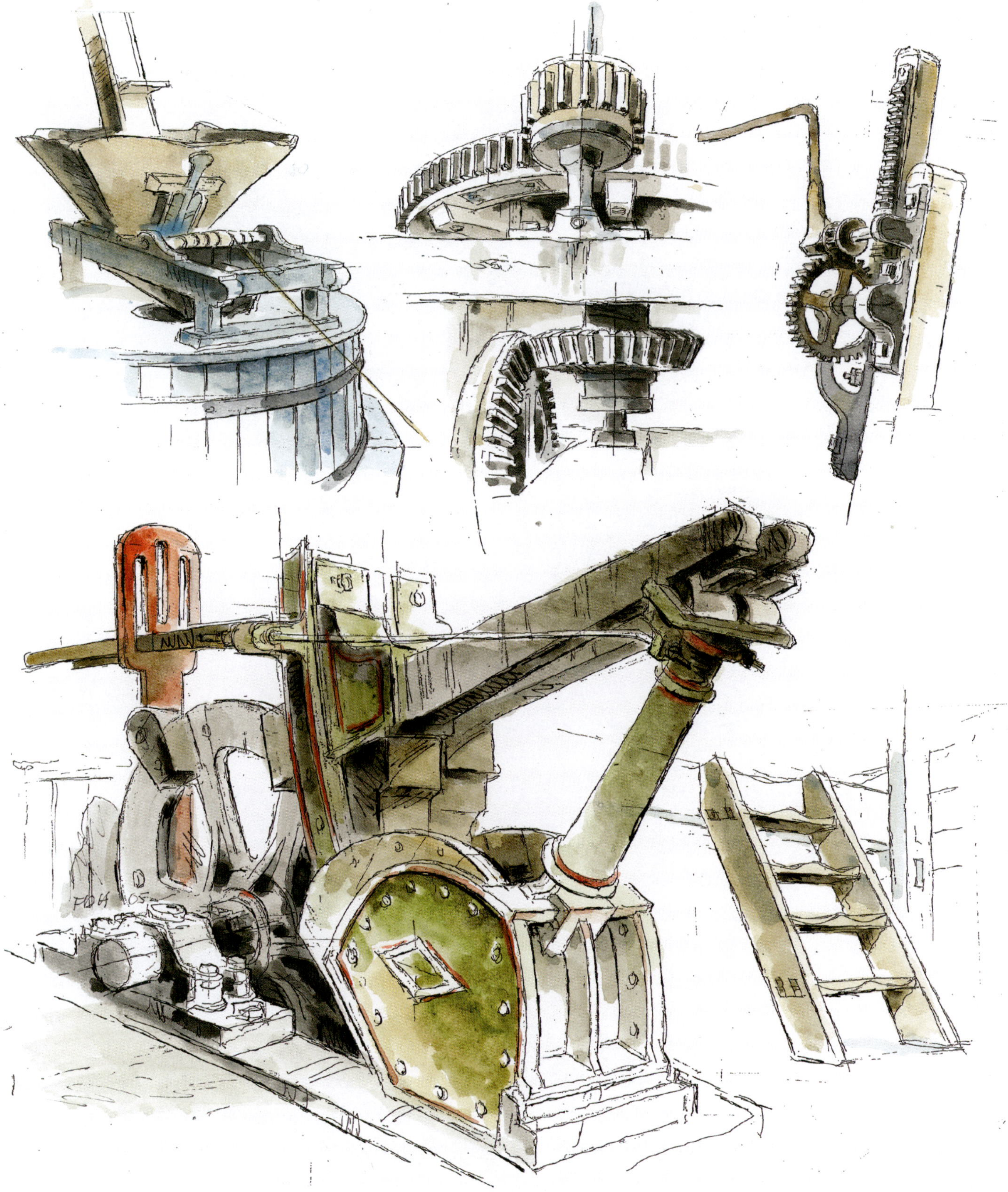

Rural Life and Industry

Industrial buildings in the countryside have attracted particular appreciation and sympathy since the rise of industrial archaeology and industrial conservation in the 1950s and 1960s. Watermills and windmills were among the very first industrial buildings to be protected, perhaps because they possessed a charm or rustic appeal not associated with the heavy industries or with urban buildings, perhaps because their technologies were more readily understood, or perhaps because they were of a scale more amenable to conservation. However, mills are far from the only representations of rural life to be appreciated, as witnessed by the enthusiasm of many owners to restore rural buildings and the establishment of folk museums such as St Fagans, Cardiff, and museums of farming like Acton Scott in Shropshire.

Falcon's drawings reinforce the point that industry in the countryside historically was not just of a few characteristic types but was vastly varied. Local industries might supply the range of local needs or exploit particular resources available in an area. As well as the ubiquitous corn mills there were small harbours that drove the fishing trade, estate gasworks and sawmills, woollen mills, cider presses and slate quarries that spread across the mountainsides of north Wales, to mention only a handful. The built heritage of some of these trades frequently expressed vernacular traditions, so that the type of limekiln or corn mill in an area can be as characteristic as its medieval church towers or its ancient farmhouses. They were often the products of accommodations between the deep past of the countryside and the rapidly changing needs and opportunities that rose out of growing trade, and they are all the more fascinating for that.

Despite the appreciation of rural industry and traditional forms of country life, however, the threat to them has been profound. Farming practices like the haymaking by hand that Falcon watched and drew in 1993 have all-but disappeared with increasing mechanisation, there is no role for small fulling mills, and coal gas has long been superseded by mains natural gas and electricity. For every corn mill that has been preserved in working order with its machinery, hundreds must have fallen into decay or been made into houses; for every harbour that still lives to the rhythm of the fishing boats, like Pittenweem, there are dozens that are now no more than holiday villages, stripped of the tough, dangerous work and stoical communities that made them.

Fulling stocks and mill machinery, 2005

In this drawing, made as a cover for the Welsh Mills Society's journal Melin, the artist brings together three subjects: a pair of millstones with their tun, horse and hopper and the gears beneath; a hand gear for raising the paddles of a canal lock; and the fulling stocks at Moelwyn woollen mill, Blaenau Ffestiniog. The last drawing shows how the two fulling mill hammers were raised and dropped alternately by the waterwheel-driven tappet wheel.

Pencil and ink on paper, 42 x 30 cm. FHA 02/15 - NPRN 40924

Stefan haymaking
15 Aug '93 FDH-5
Pen-y-bryn, Blaenau Ffestiniog

Woolshop for retail of the mill's products to be rebuilt, with access to rear at left, & flat for the owner over of same plan as on drawing No.119/5/2.

Falcon D Hildred, Pant-y-pwll Mill, Bl. Ffestiniog
Drawing No. 119/5/3 October '94
Scale: 1/8" + 3/16 = 1'-0"

Showing proposed restoration of mill & shop to full working order.

Prepared on behalf of the owner Bleddyn Jones Esq.

The shrinking stock

- The mill & property as a whole
- owner's flat
- garaging for 3 cars (there is also off the road parking for 3 more)
- suggested car-park, railway hall, & riverside walk for visitors
- alternative parking for 8 cars if mill leat culverted

grid ref: 691455

The restful, unplanned modest & unpretentious character

Moelwyn Woollen Mill, Tanygrisiau, Gwynedd

Stefan haymaking, Pen-y-Bryn, Blaenau Ffestiniog, 1993

Falcon drew this scene of haymaking at his neighbour's farm from his sitting room window using binoculars on the morning of 18 August 1993. Stefan, the farmer, had been a German prisoner of war in the area and decided to stay on when peace came. He always did his haymaking by the traditional method of clearing the edge with a scythe and then bringing the tractor in with family and friends to cut the middle. It turned out to be the last time he cut the meadow this way.

Pencil, ink and watercolour on paper, 15 x 26 cm.
FHA 01/108 - NPRN 305760

Moelwyn mill, Tan-y-grisiau, 1972

This is one of a number of drawings made to support proposals for the restoration and part-conversion of Moelwyn mill, the only woollen mill in Wales to retain its fulling stocks for finishing cloth. This version proposes the addition of a shop at the end of the mill house with a small flat above and a scheme to retain the machinery as a working museum and to provide an outlet for the mill's products. Falcon's interest helped to get the mill listed and Gwynedd Council restored the mill and its machinery in the 1970s, but it remains vulnerable.

Ink, candle wax and watercolour on wrapping paper, 27 x 62 cm
FHA 01/050 - NPRN 40924

Cider house, Cwm Farm, Llangattock Lingoed, Monmouthshire, 2007

Falcon recorded this building during a visit by the Welsh Mills Society. The lower view is looking through the front wall. Cider mill components are often retained as garden features, but this one is still complete after more than 250 years. The purpose-built cider house was completed in 1754 by William Watkins, whose initials are recorded on the date-stone above the door. The cider press has a screw carved from a single piece of wood and there is an apple loft with a stone-lined chute down which apples were fed to the mill.

Ink and watercolour drawing on paper, 29 x 42 cm.
FHA 02/10 - NPRN 407523

Parc Glynllifon estate workshops - steam engine and saws, 1995

Glynllifon, a few miles south-west of Caernarfon, was the family seat of the Wynn family, Barons Newborough. The estate workshops date from about 1830 and were laid out according to the best practices of the time. The four corner drawings show the boiler house, the horizontal steam engine, the vertical multi-blade saw that cut whole trees into planks and the slate mill with a table saw. In the centre the artist shows each component in the buildings, drawn transparently so as to show the pipes and drive belts between them.

Digital print, 42 x 30 cm. FHA 02/50/02 - NPRN 31381

Windmill, Coventry, undated

This early drawing, from the 1960s, uses dark skies and dead, blackened vegetation to highlight the dereliction and decay of this tower windmill at Rowington. The imagery is more deeply Neo-Romantic than any of Falcon's later work. The mill was known at Bouncing Bess; two others in the parish, now disappeared, were Grinning Jenny and Tom o' the Wood. The three-storey brick tower was built before 1789 and worked until 1916; in 1978 it was converted into a house.

Ink and watercolour on paper, 11 x 7 cm.
FHA 03/54

Hayloft at Acton Scott farming museum, Shropshire, 1980

Acton Scott was the first farming museum of its kind in Britain, dedicated to keeping alive the rural practices of the late nineteenth century. It preserves many traditions that might otherwise have been lost. It is known to many as a setting for the 2009 BBC documentary series, Victorian Farm. Here the artist's eye is drawn to the simple lines and materials of an eighteenth-century farm building, depicted in isolation yet forming an integral element of an estate worked by heavy horses.

Pencil, ink and watercolour on paper, 17 x 20 cm. FHA 03/73

Cellardyke harbour, Scotland, 1984

Cellardyke is one of several historic fishing ports in Fife, on the north coast of the Firth of Forth. Its heyday was in the 1860s, when more than two hundred boats were based here; many were lost in a disastrous storm in 1898. In this sketch, made on site, the artist records the almost deserted harbour, and some of the narrow streets of historic buildings clustered around it. Now the growth of neighbouring Anstruther has engulfed this picturesque settlement.

Pencil and watercolour on paper, 23 x 30 cm. FHA 04/01/01

Pittenweem, Scotland - The Giles, 1984

The Giles, or Gyles, encloses the east end of Pittenweem's harbour, the safest of the East Neuk of Fife's fishing ports. Its pre-eminence has been strengthened by a new fish market, but in this drawing from 1984 Falcon shows earlier days, when boxes of fish were moved about on handcarts and stacked on the quayside on numbered paving slabs to be sold in strict rotation according to the order of return of the boats. Falcon notes that the town was constructed to be pleasing even though it was a working settlement. The crow-stepped gables and red pantiled roofs reaffirm the former importance of fish exports to the Low Countries.

Coloured line copy, 30 x 21 cm. FHA 0411/02

Pittenweem, Scotland - solitary building with fishermen and light, 1984

This simple subject, set on a fragment of Fife's rocky coast, epitomises the classic building style of the fishing villages of the East Neuk, with crow-stepped gables echoing the architecture of the Low Countries. Pantiles also came from the Low Countries, as ballast in the boats trading in smoked and dried fish, and they became the characteristic roofing material on both sides of the Firth of Forth. Are the fishermen reminiscing about the past glories of the fishing industry?

Coloured line copy, 30 x 21 cm.
FHA 04/09/02

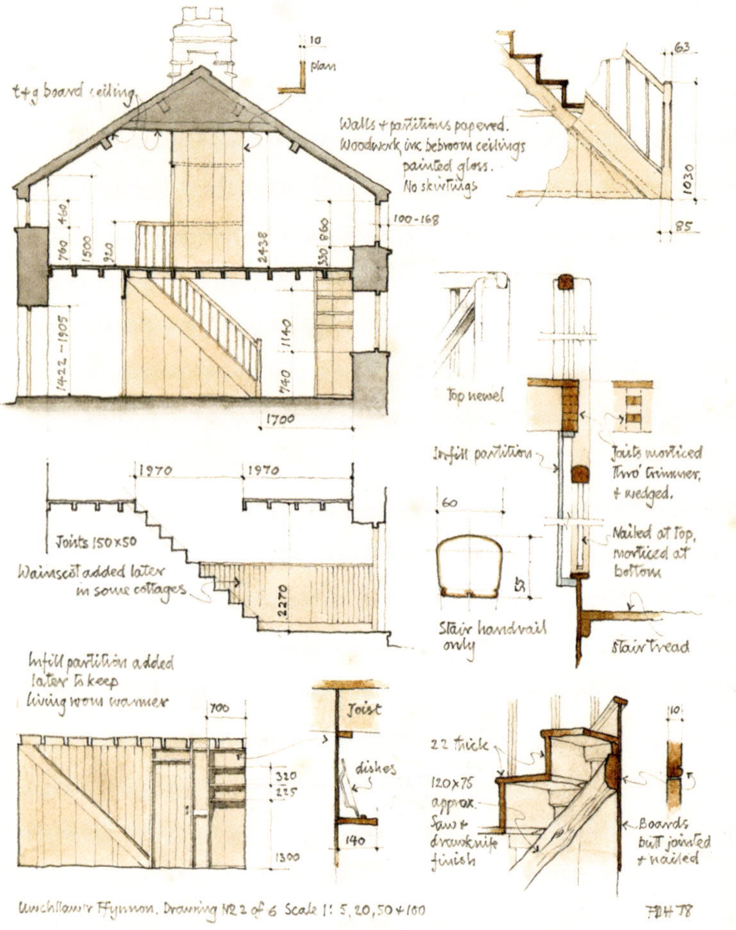
t+g board ceiling
10
plan
Walls + partitions papered.
Woodwork inc bedroom ceilings
painted gloss.
No skirtings
63
1030
85
100-168
760
460
500
920
2438
330
860
1140
740
1422-1905
1700
Top newel
Infill partition
Joists morticed
thro' trimmer,
+ wedged.
60
Nailed at top,
morticed at
bottom
Stair handrail
only
Stair tread
1970
1970
Joists 150x50
Wainscot added later
in some cottages
2270
Infill partition added
later to keep
living room warmer
700
Joist
dishes
320
235
1300
140
22 thick
120x75
approx.
Saw +
drawknife
finish
10
Boards
butt jointed
+ nailed
Uwchllaw'r Ffynnon. Drawing No 2 of 6 Scale 1: 5, 20, 50 + 100
FDH 78

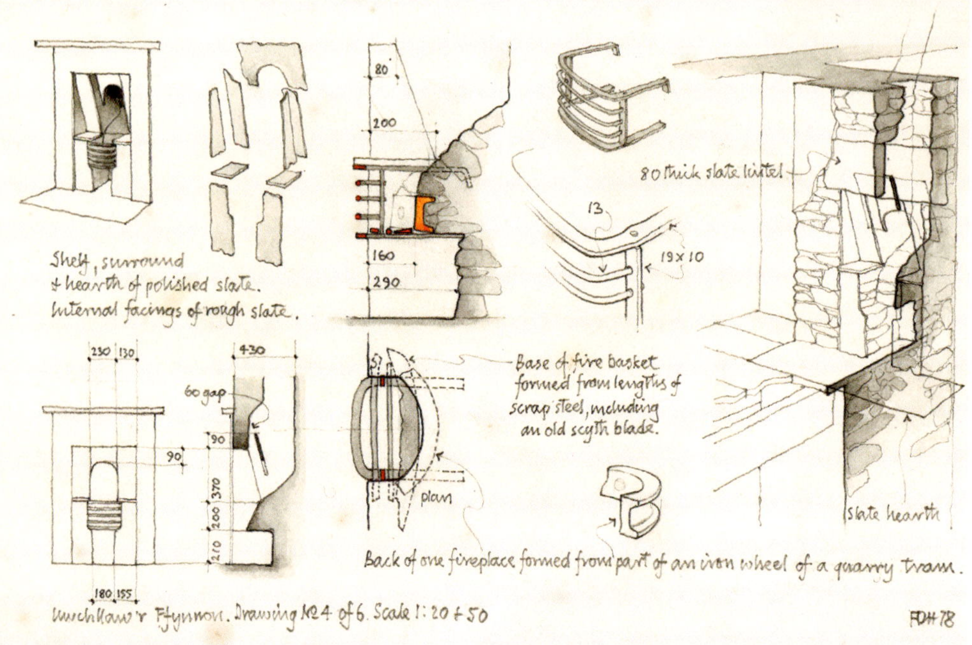
80
200
160
290
Shelf, surround
+ hearth of polished slate.
Internal facings of rough slate.
13
19x10
80 thick slate lintel
230
130
430
60 gap
90
90
370
200
210
180
155
Base of fire basket
formed from lengths of
scrap steel, including
an old scyth blade.
plan
Slate hearth
Back of one fireplace formed from part of an iron wheel of a quarry tram.
Uwchllaw'r Ffynnon. Drawing No 4 of 6. Scale 1: 20 + 50
FDH 78

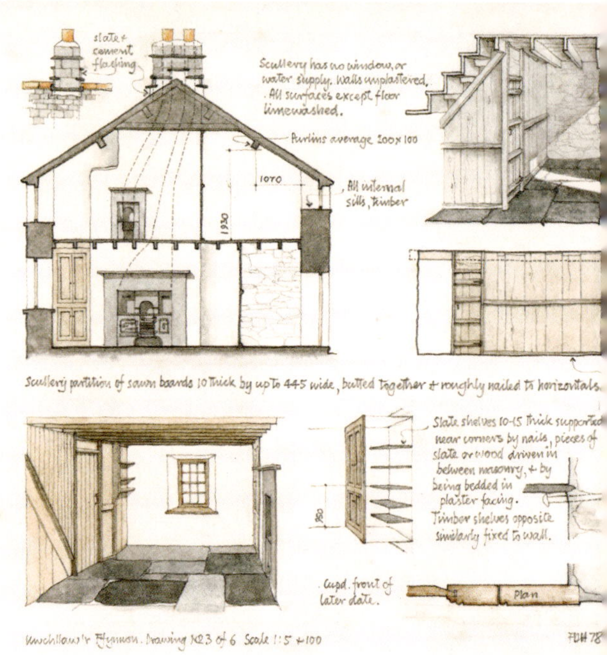
slate +
cement
flashing
Scullery has no window or
water supply. Walls unplastered.
All surfaces except floor
limewashed.
Purlins average 200x100
1070
All internal
sills, timber
1930
Scullery partition of sawn boards 10 thick by up to 445 wide, butted together + roughly nailed to horizontals.
Slate shelves 10-15 thick supported
near corners by nails, pieces of
slate or wood driven in
between masonry, + by
being bedded in
plaster facing.
Timber shelves opposite
similarly fixed to wall.
380
Cupd. front of
later date.
Plan
Uwchllaw'r Ffynnon. Drawing No 3 of 6 Scale 1:5 + 100
FDH 78

My Working Process
by Falcon Hildred[16]

I see everything through the eyes of a designer. From infancy I was curious about how things got their shape and what they did. So I was fascinated by the signal boxes, maltings, gasworks, dockland cranes and way of life of my childhood surroundings. And from infancy I loved drawing.

Looking back now, therefore, it seems clear to me that I most probably came into the world already programmed to record some of the last remnants of the nineteenth and early twentieth century working-class scenery and life. The work of recording began in 1960, when, after fifteen years of post-war redevelopment and change, the scenery and way of life of my childhood was rapidly disappearing; being destroyed, often indiscriminately, good as well as bad, and not always replaced with something better. I found it very upsetting.

Not that the old way of life had much to commend it. It was for the most part muck, hard work and ugliness. Yet there was nothing bland and faint-hearted about it. It had power, character, vitality and integrity. And it was these qualities I found exciting and felt compelled in some way to show my respect for.

Despite all our prejudices and easy criticisms, commerce and industry achieved more in two centuries to transform and improve the lives of every ordinary person than everything throughout our entire history. And this social revolution did not just come down from higher minds, it came up from the grime and relentless exploitation and suffering of those ordinary people. And the place where this most worthy battle was fought and won, was the British nineteenth-century industrial town.

In setting the project up, I decided on four things. First, the title: Worktown. Second, that none of the drawings would be for sale. Everything would be held together as a record, which meant that I had to keep working as a designer and part-time teacher in order to live. Third, that subjects would be anything appropriate and interesting from a tin shed to, as I found later, a whole town. And finally, that the period of study would be from my own living memory, with only a brief acknowledgement of such places as pre-industrial fishing towns, through to demolition but not beyond. Choice of subject and location were quite haphazard. If I came across something of interest in my travels, then I would sketch it or maybe go back to do so. Mostly though, choice was governed by where I was working or living, which explains why Grimsby, Coventry, London and Blaenau Ffestiniog feature prominently.

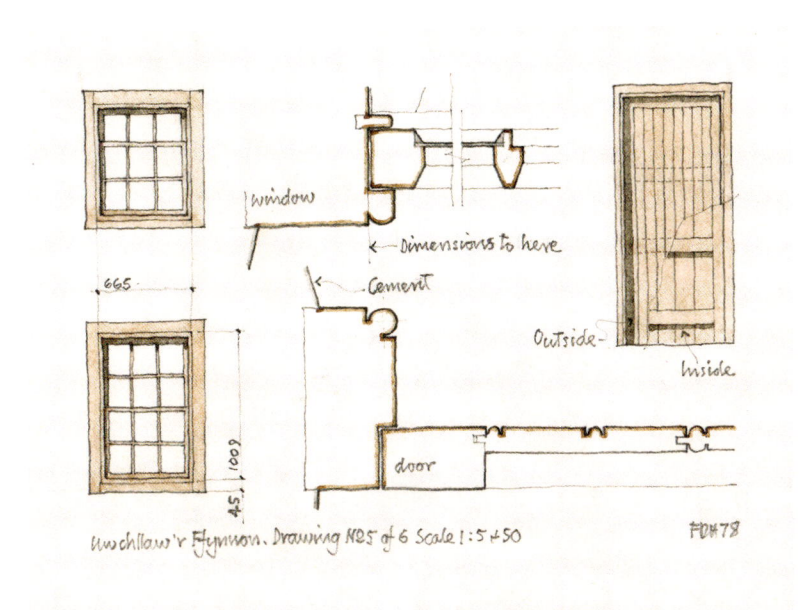

Uwchllaw'r Ffynnon, 1978

Some of the six drawings that make up a set documenting a terrace of houses very close to Falcon's mill at Blaenau Ffestiniog. The plan and elevation are on page 76. The drawings are thorough in their detail, from floors to rooftops, fireplaces to window glazing-bars. Presented as technical drawings, they would be sufficient to reconstruct a replica of the buildings, but they also capture eloquently the cottages' character. The approach can be compared with a series of photographs taken by the Royal Commission in 1975.

Pencil and watercolour on paper, 18 x 14.5, 11 x 16, 18 x 15, 18 x 12 cm.
Drawings: FHA01/112-115, *Photograph*: DI2009_0969 - NPRN 28882

Fort Belan harbour, 1997

This series of persectives and details of the 1820s defensive harbour at the western entrance to the Menai Strait allows Falcon to 'take the viewer on a tour'.

Pencil, ink and watercolour on paper, 42 x 30 cm.
FHA02/67/10 - NPRN 26459

Site sketches of Fort Belan, 1997

These multiple sketches represent the artist gathering information for one of his composite drawings of the fort at Fort Belan, see page 35.

Pencil on paper, 23 x 37 cm. FHA 02/07/07 - NPRN 26459

Cardiff and Newport were commissions, as was the study I made of Overton village, where I adopted for the first time the method of starting at the 30 mile speed limit to get the traveller's first impression, then move inwards to see the place in more detail.

The next thing then was to decide what style of illustration to use to present each subject in the most appropriate way. Thus a measured drawing was used for the chimney (page 40), and something more painterly for the shop (frontispiece). Others like Eli Green's Cottage Factory (pages 156-161) required a mix of both. Many subjects require a whole series of drawings, often with several views on each sheet, in order to show everything of interest. I call these drawings composites or sometimes picture maps as in the case of Fort Belan harbour, where I then take the viewer on a tour of what's there to see.

The ultimate in terms of complexity and involving the techniques of map-making, technical illustration and writing, were the books on Newport Transporter Bridge and *A Word in your Eye*. So, depending on what I decided was needed, works ranged from a simple sketch knocked out in minutes during a journey, to something taking several years of research and preparation.

From the outset it was the pace of demolition that drove the work along and governed choice. If something was interesting but safe, I would leave it. But if it was about to go, I would record it. Often there was so much coming down and so little time in which to respond, that all I could do was get the information down quickly, then draw it up later, often several years later, which is why some drawings have two dates.

Photography would seem to have been the obvious solution, and although I took many slides, they rarely gave me the results I wanted. Also there was the inconvenient delay in waiting for the film to be developed, and anyway I just couldn't work from photographs. To really understand the subject I had to draw it.

The first essential therefore in every case was to make a site sketch. This would tell me whether the subject really was worthy of record and if so why? Whether it would make an interesting picture and from what angle? What may be the best way of dealing with the subject – measured drawing or something atmospheric? And generally how I felt about it? Thus a relationship had begun that was sometimes completed there and then, sometimes years later, and sometimes never taken any further.

Most of my site studies have an 's' after the date (to note that they were drawn on site), and often they're the best or as good as need be. Not everything needs to be meticulously finished, through a lot of my site drawings are. In drawing outside from life there's no time for messing about, so there's no editing and I never use artistic licence. No need. The truth is interesting enough. Though I will sometimes go beneath the surface to understand a detail or show something of interest. Two advantages in addition to getting the job done quickly, are that with having the subject in front of you, it's possible to be really quite accurate. And finally, drawings done under these conditions can often have more spontaneity and vitality than something produced on a drawing board. I've sometimes laboured over a finished drawing, only to tear it up as soon as it's finished. There's enough rubbish in the world without adding more.

Whether working outside on site or at home on the drawing board, drawing is where the hard work is done and everything sorted out: contents, composition, perspective and so on. On a drawing board job this can mean spending a lot of time on preliminaries – rather like learning and practising a piece of music. But once this stage is over, the finished drawing is usually fairly quickly produced.

Colouring the drawing afterwards is also relatively quick and generally easier too. But I find it's not until this is done that the picture takes on solidity and comes to life. Then finally the best bit:

Bryntirion, Blaenau Ffestiniog, 1987

This brief sketch is an example of how an image made on site can capture all the essential information about a building quite efficiently – in this case the scale and type of an isolated cottage and the way it sits in rough moorland on the edge of the quarry landscapes.

Pencil and watercolour on paper, 21 x 29.5 cm.
FHA01/084 - NPRN 416029

adding the mount. A mount can transform even the most modest work.

The majority of the drawings are in pencil or ink with watercolour on cartridge, which means that correctly speaking they are watercolour drawings, though a few are watercolour paintings. Some of the darker pictures are chalk and ink, and I have had some lovely results on brown wrapping paper. The reasons for drawing rather than painting or using chalk, are many fold. First, it requires only two simple things, pencil and paper; it's quick, dry and clean; it can cope with detail; and it's versatile, particularly when used with a drawing board. A drawing board allows the freedom to range between technical drawings using a set square and scale rule, maps, drawings that dissect, illustrate and explain by using x-ray vision or cutaways, straightforward views, sketch details and explanatory notes, right through to title and even a border if need be.

Historically, such drawings are in the tradition developed by architects, engineers and others presenting their ideas. They are drawings which require a good sense of order and an understanding of form, space, construction, perspective, light and shade; also an ability to convey all of this reliably and realistically, without any fudging or becoming tedious. They are compact, clear and complete, and beautiful too, works of art in their own right.

An important part of my work is knowing where to stop, which is why most of my drawings are vignettes. As soon as I've said what I want to say, I fade the drawing out. So there's often no sky, and very little foreground or surroundings.

We've all been to places or had experiences which have created an impression that has lasted, maybe even haunted us long after. Some of my favourite memories are of exploring buildings that had been abandoned and left open to the elements and nature. Their silence seemed to crave a sympathetic listener.

Back in the early 'seventies, I once had to do a winter train journey across the Pennines from Manchester to Leeds. Darkness had fallen and it had snowed. There were delays and cancellations, the train was packed and there was neither heating nor light. Every seat was taken so I had to sit on my rucksack at the end of the corridor in the darkness and cold. It should have been a thoroughly miserable journey, but instead it was totally enchanting. As the train crawled along, we passed through a winter wonderland of small Pennine towns lit up, and with their mills and chimneys, viaducts and huddled houses all silhouetted against the snow and softly lit

Moelwyn Mill, design showing part-conversion to flat, 1973

An example of Falcon's combination of different approaches to visualisation on one image, with cutaways, perspectives, interior details and plans.

Pencil and watercolour on paper, 42 x 30 cm.
FHA02/40/01 - NPRN 40924

night sky. I had a perfect view all the way, through an open window with no-one to complain. And if I could book that journey again, I would. But of course it's all changed now.

Even when old buildings are saved and smartened up or adapted to a new use – which is good, I no longer feel the urge to draw them once they're out of their working clothes. It's got to be the full works for me: mood as well as masonry. So, many of my drawings are a way of preserving the unpreservable.

And although people feature only modestly in my pictures, they are the very fountain head of what I do.

So what conclusions do I draw from all of this? Has there been any advancement of knowledge? Any lessons learned? Do I have any closing artist's statement to make, or plan to unfold? My answer to all these is yes. Being a designer, I don't see my pictures as just something to be passively enjoyed. They're not just a record, but a vision too, so they have a job to do.

The central aims of my first Worktown exhibition in 1976 was to encourage a more appreciative attitude towards our industrial towns. This is still my aim, even though almost everything I've drawn has since gone. But not everything has gone in Blaenau, not yet. But it is going and changing, slowly maybe, but relentlessly.

After half a century of recording, I believe that Blaenau Ffestiniog and its landscape are the best and most complete surviving industrial landscape in Britain. Over the last few years it has been the inspiration for my biggest worktown study – a portrait of a whole community as seen through the town and landscape which it created. A man-made, hand-made landscape of around 16 square miles (27km) that is one of the richest concentrations of industrial remains in Britain.

This is the landscape that attracted me to Blaenau. That is why I moved into an old slate mill here, and that's what inspired my pictures. But now look at this in reverse. Starting with the pictures, then the mill, the town and finally the landscape – looking towards the bigger picture, the whole. That is what I would like to see properly valued and cared for. I feel we should save one example of a nineteenth-century industrial town as a complete cultural and historic entity. So my final message is: if you like my pictures, then please take care of the subject that inspired them.

To my mother and father, Rita and Carole.
Falcon, 11 October 2012

Finding out more

All images from the Falcon Hildred Collection in the National Monuments Record of Wales are available for consultation in the Royal Commission's offices in Aberystwyth. Digital copies are also held at Ironbridge Gorge Museum. Further information about the sites in Wales can be found online at *www.coflein.gov.uk*, which can be searched by site details or using the National Primary Record Number (NPRN) listed in picture captions. A selection of images is also available online through People's Collection Wales, *www.peoplescollection.co.uk*, including works held by Newport Museum and Art Gallery.

A short film, *Falcon Hildred*, made for the Royal Commission by Pete Telfer of Culture Colony based on interviews with the artist can be seen online.

Notes

1 All quotations in this book, unless stated otherwise, come from Falcon Hildred's interview with the author recorded at Melin Pant-yr-ynn, Blaenau Ffestiniog, in 2011, filmed by Pete Telfer. Parts of the interview have been used in the film commissioned by the Royal Commission, and copies of this and the full audio recording are held in the National Monuments Record of Wales.

2 Falcon Hildred, statement, August 2012.

3 Falcon Hildred, statement, August 2012.

4 Personal communication from Falcon Hildred to Peter Wakelin; J. Geraint Jenkins, 1969, *The Welsh woollen industry*, Cardiff, pp. 207-10 refers to the woollen mill being built in 1813 but does not record its known period as a slab mill; David Gwyn, 2006, *Gwynedd: Inheriting a revolution*, Chichester, pp. 50 and 122 refers to it as being built by Diffwys quarry as a slate mill between 1844 and 1847.

5 Falcon Hildred, statement, August 2012.

6 The Royal Commission would be keen to hear from owners of any of these drawings who might be willing for copies to be made available alongside the rest of the archive.

7 Falcon D. Hildred, *Newport Transporter Bridge: A Guide to its History, Construction and Operation* (Newport: Newport Borough Council, 1996).

8 Falcon D. Hildred 2004. *Industrial Heritage* 30, 1, Spring 2004.

9 Falcon Hildred, statement, August 2012.

10 Falcon Hildred, note to Peter Wakelin, 14 February 2012.

11 Personal communication from Falcon HIldred to Peter Wakelin, August 2012.

12 David Mellor 1987. *A Paradise Lost: the Neo-Romantic imagination in Britain 1935-55*, London: Lund Humphries; Peter Wakelin 1998. 'Bert Isaac', *Modern Painters*, Autumn 1998, p. 116.

13 The phrase comes from the title of the moving orchestral fanfare by the American composer Aaron Copeland, written in 1942 to mark the entry of the United States into the Second World War.

14 Falcon Hildred, statement, August 2012.

15 Falcon Hildred, statement on the Blaenau landscape, August 2012.

16 This chapter is an edited version of a handwritten account provided by Falcon Hildred titled 'Why and how I went about recording', dated 16 June 2012. A copy of this and a typed transcript are held in the National Monuments Record.

Acknowledgements

The Falcon Hildred Access and Learning Project has been made possible by a grant from the Heritage Lottery Fund and we are grateful for their support throughout the process, particularly the case officer John Bryon.

Many staff at the Royal Commission have taken part in the work for this publication or the supporting activities. Rachael Barnwell, Hilary Malaws and Peter Wakelin co-ordinated the project with support from Gareth Edwards, Scott Lloyd and Angharad Williams. Fleur James digitised the entire collection of drawings, Iain Wright recorded photographically Falcon's home at Blaenau Ffestiniog. The collection was catalogued by Lynne Moore. Additional caption text was researched and contributed by Rachael Barnwell, Susan Fielding, Daniel Jones, Scott Lloyd, Brian Malaws and, in a voluntary capacity, John Crompton, formerly of the National Museum of Scotland, who also prepared site information for Coflein. Helen Rowe prepared material for People's Collection Wales. Penny Icke assisted with copyright issues. The book was designed by John Johnston and its production was assisted by Patricia Moore and Stephen Bailey John. Nicola Roberts assisted with the promotion of the collection.

The Ironbridge Gorge Museum Trust have been the principal additional partner in the project since its inception. We would like to thank The Trust's Director Steve Miller, alongside Lucy Andrews-Marion, Paul Gossage, Anna Brennand, David de Haan, Matthew Thompson and volunteers who have prepared outreach and engagement work using the collection.

Numerous other partners have participated in the project. Newport Museum and Art Gallery have provided images from their collection and we are particularly grateful to Mike Lewis and Oliver Blackmore, and to former staff Roger Cucksey and Robin Hawkins. Exhibitions of the collection will be shown there and at the National Library of Wales and the North Wales Slate Museum in Llanberis, part of Amgueddfa Cymru – National Museum Wales. Pete Telfer of Culture Colony made a film to support the exhibition and add to the permanent documentation of the collection.

The text of the book was read and commented on by David de Haan, Falcon Hildred, Tom Lloyd, Dr Eurwyn Wiliam, Professor Christopher Williams.

We are deeply grateful to Sir Neil Cossons for his foreword and to Falcon Hildred for his constant support.

Index

Note: Page numbers in *italic* refer to illustrations and captions.

Abercynon 33; miners' institute 37, *37*
Aberglaslyn 19
Acton Scott farming museum 183, *189*
agricultural show 37
Albany Road, Coventry *87*
Albert Dock 127, *135*
allotments *110*
almshouses *84*
Andrew Knight Gallery 29, *146*
Angel, The, Newport *104*
arcades *56*
Armstrong, William *149*
Arnodin, Ferdinand *140*

Baedeker Raid 15
Bailey dry dock, Newport *138*
baked potato cart 62, *63*
Bardsey Island *49*
Bellevue Park, Newport *71*
Bennion, Caroline *84*
Bethania 9, *10*, 22, *76*
Bethania chapel, Blaenau Ffestiniog 117, *123-25*
Bethesda 165
Birmingham 62, *63*; college of art 15, *16*
Blackdown mill 46, *154*
Blaenau Ffestiniog 7, 9, 10, 11, 12-13, *12*, 21–23, 28–29, *31*, 51, *52–55*, 75, *78-79*, 193, *196*, 198, 204; chapels 117, *118*, *120-21*, *123-25*; coal office *142*, 143; cottages 37, *76-83*, 94; High Street *53*, 174, *175*; library 99, *100*; market hall 28, *29*, *42–43*, *102*; school *100*; slate 165-81; town centre 30; transport 127, *128*
Bonc Goedai winding house *176*
Bratby, John 46
breweries *147*
bridges 4, *5*, *6*, *7*, 69, *73*, *126*, 127, *132*, 133, *136*, *137*
Bryntirion, Blaenau Ffestiniog *196*
Byker Bridge, Newcastle *6*, *7*, *136*, *137*

Caernarfon 34, *187*
Caerphilly Castle 34
Cambridge 22
canals 127, *134*
Cardiff 13, 29, *56-57*, *86*, 146, 195; brewery *147*; food factory *145*; library *41*; prison *106*; pubs *103*; theatre *103*; YMCA *105*
Cash, J.J. 7, *40*, 41

Cellardyke harbour *190*
chapels 116-25
Charleston 22
Charlton 7, *18-19*, 19, *62*, 75, *90-93*, *110*
Chepstow Road, Newport *97*
Chester 13
chimneys 7, *40*, 41, *149*
Christo 47
churches 116-25
cider mill 186
cinemas 99, *112*
Cleethorpes 13, 60, *61*
Clifton Road, Westminster 94
Cobden Treaty 38
Colne, River *60-61*
commercial buildings 99-115
Copeland, Aaron 199
Corporation Road school, Newport 69
Corris 165
corrugated iron 11, *12*
cottage factory 37-38, 75, *156-61*, 195
cottages 10, *76*, *78-83*, *85*, 94
Courtybella Terrace, Newport *96*
Coventry 2, 4, 7, 13, 19, 29, 40, 41, 46, 48, 64, 75, 89, 193; art school 15, *150*; Blitz 15, 38, *40*; canal *134*; cathedral 15, *16*; cottage factory 37–38, 75, *156-61*; factories *150*, *152*; houses *87*, *88*; school *109*; silk ribbon weaving 37–38, *150*, *155-61*; watchmaking *155-56*; windmill *188*
Craxton, John 46
Crimea pass *166*
Croesor incline *178*
Cucksey, Roger 32
Cwm Croesor *178*
Cwm Farm, Llangattock Lingoed *186*
Cwm Penmachno *179*

Deiniolen 165
Deptford Mill *65*
Diffwys Casson quarry *176*
Diffwys quarry 23, *174*, 199
docks *135*
Dorothea quarry 46, *47*
Dover Street school, Coventry *109*
Dowlais: ironworks 143; stables *148*
drawing *vs* camera 43–45
drum-houses 11, *11*

Eastport 66
Ebenezer chapel, Merthyr Tydfil 119
Ede, Jim 22
Elwyn, John 46
Emerson Chambers, Newcastle 107
engineering 126-41
Evans, Gareth J. 19

factories 37–38, 40, 41, 145
Falkland 66
farming 183, 184, 185, 189
Farr & Reddy grocers 64
ferries 137
Ffestiniog railway 28, 55, 173, 179
Fife 67
filtration tower 133
fishing 183
food factory 145
Fort Belan 34, 34, 35, 194-95, 195
Foty and Bowydd quarry 164, 165
Four Crosses 53
Fox Street, Birmingham 62, 63
fulling stocks 182, 183
furniture 15, 17

Garreg Flaen-llyn 169, 173
gas works 144, 151
Glamorgan library 41
Glan y Don slate tip 128
Glanypwll Road 52
Gloddfa Ganol cottages 94
Gorllwyn-uchaf 85
Graig Nyth-y-Gigfran 169
Grangetown 86, 105
Green, Eli 37–38, 75, 156-61, 195
Grimsby 1, 7, 13, 13, 14-15, 29, 38, 60, 61, 151, 162, 193
Grimshaw, John Atkinson 37
Guest, Josiah John 148
Gwydr House, Overton-on-Dee 59
Gwylfa chapel, Blaenau Ffestiniog 118

Habershon, Pite and Fawkner 122
hallhouse 85
harbours 183, 190-91, 194
Hartley, Jesse 127, 135
Havelock Street chapel, Newport 122
Hawkesbury lock 134
haymaking 183, 184, 185
Haynes, Robert 140
Hepworth, Barbara 22
Hertford Square, Coventry 7, 74, 75

Hildred, Falcon: bedsit 19, 20; birthplace 1; book on design 34, 43; childhood 13-15; drawing 43–47; early career 19-21; education 15-19; national service 17; working process 193-98
Hildred, Trevlynn 15
Hildred-Evans Industrial Design 18, 19
Hockney, David 43
Holland's level 52, 170-73; slate mill 173; slate mine 94-95
Holyhead road 133
houses 74–97
housing demolition 10, 21, 74, 75
Hull 13, 137
Humber ferries 137
hydraulic power 149

ice cream vendor 108
inclines 174, 176, 178, 180
industrial buildings 142-63
industrial museums 143
industrial towns 51
Inkpot House see Tŷ Uncorn
Ipswich 153
Ireland, Rita 19, 21, 173, 198
ironworks 148, 163
Isaac, Bert 46, 47
Isaac Lord, Ipswich 153

Jacquard looms 159-60
Jones, David 46
Jones, Jacob and Son 23, 176
Jones, R.L. and Son 11, 12, 12
Jones, Robert Lloyd 118

Kettle's Yard, Cambridge 22

Lancashire 163
Landsdowne Lane, Charlton 18-19, 19, 62, 75, 90-92
Leamington Spa 154
level crossings 13, 55
libraries 41, 98, 99, 100, 101
library furniture 17
Lime Street, Newcastle 6, 7
limekilns 183
Lincoln Castle, PS 137
Liverpool 127, 135
Llanberis 165
Llangattock Lingoed 186
Llanthony Priory 34
Llanwern steelworks 69
Llechwedd quarry 128, 130, 166
London 7, 13, 17-19, 38, 50, 51, 62, 65, 75, 90-94, 110, 193
Long, Richard 47
Lord Street 204
Lydford Street, Woolwich 39
Lydgate 163
Llyn Bowydd dam 179

Madoc quarry *32*
Madocks, William 117
Maenofferen quarry *44–45*, 165, *180-81*; winding house *180*
manager's house 77
Manod *118*; Mawr *179*; mountain 22; granite quarry 32; school *101*
Melin Pant-yr-ynn *see* Pant-yr-ynn
Menai Bridge 4, 5, *68*, 69, *126*, 127
Merthyr Tydfil 33, *119*, 143, *148*
mill town *163*
mills *8, 9, 10, 22*, 22–28, 36, 43, 46, *65, 154*, 183, *185, 186*; machinery *182*, 183
miners' institutes 99
Minton, John 46
Moderator wharf, Newport *138-39*
Modernism 17, *18*
Moelwyn, hills 22, *25*;
Moelwyn mill 23, 28, *36, 182*, 183, *185, 197*
Monet, Claude 46
monoloco *130*
Morgan Arcade, Cardiff *56*
Morris, Owen *102*
Morris, Richard *130*
municipal baths 99, *111*
museums 183
music hall *57*
Muslim Cultural Centre, Grangetown *105*

Nantlle 46, *47*, 165
Nash, David 23
National Schools Society 99
New Cross 21
Newcastle upon Tyne 6, 7, 13, 29, *107, 136*, 137, *149*; wash house *111*
Newport 13, 32–33, 51, *69–73, 96-97*, 112, 195; chapels *122*; docks *138-39*; hotel *115*; ironworks *163*; library *98*, 99; market *112*; medieval ship *138*; public conveniences *114*; pubs *104*; Transporter Bridge 33–34, *140-41*, 195

Oakley quarries *128, 166, 168*, 169, *173*, 176
Octopus Bridge, Newport 73
office furniture *18*
Ogwen Falls *132*, 133
Ouseburn Valley 7, *136*, 137
Overton-on-Dee *58–59, 84*, 195
Owen, Tommy 10

PC's food and drink factory *145*
Pant-y-Celyn *54*, 55
Pant yr Afon 127, *128-29*
Pant-yr-ynn mill *8, 9, 10, 22*, 22–28, 46, *174, 176*, 199
pantiles *191*

Parc Glynllifon 34, *187*; gas works *144*
Park Street Shop, Coventry 2, 4
parks 71
Pasture Street, Grimsby *1*; crossing *13*
Penhevad Street, Grangetown *86*
Penrhyn 165
Pen-y-Bryn farm *183*, 184
Penygroes 10, 165
Perpendicular architecture *15, 16*
Philharmonic music hall, Cardiff *57*
Pike, Joseph 13
Pillgwenlly, Newport *98*, 99, *114, 163*
Piper, John 15, 46, *46*
Pittenweem harbour 190, *191*
Prenteg 85
Price, Arthur J. *112*
Prince of Wales theatre, Cardiff 57, *103*
prisons 99, *106*
Prospect Vale, London 7, *93, 110*
public buildings 99-115
public conveniences *114*
public houses 99, *103, 104*, 115
Putney 19, *20*

quarries *9, 11*, 23, 32, *44–45, 47*, 128, *165-81*, 199

railways *13*, 28, 55, 127
rear yards *90*, 92
Rhiw-bach quarry *11*; tramway 179
Rhiw chapel 23, *52*
Rhiwbrifidr *52*
Rhosydd drum house *178*; quarry 178
Richards, Ceri 46
Roberts, Owen *102*
rock cannon 169
rocking chair *15*
Rotherham and Son, Coventry *152*
Rowington *188*
Royal College of Art *15*, 17

St Fagans 183
St Ives 22
schools 99, *108-109*
Seaton Delaval 46
Shearman, Carole 25, *198*
Ship Inn, Newcastle 6, 7
ship interiors *17, 18*
shops 2, 4, *64*, 99, *110*
Sickert, Walter Richard 46
silk ribbon weaving 37–38, *150, 155-61*
Simpson, Benjamin *107*
slate 164-81; mills *9*; mining *11*; quarries *9*; tips *128*

Snowdonia National Park 21
Snowdonia Society 165
Sorrell, Alan 46, *154*
Spence, Sir Basil *16*
Spiller's warehouse, Cardiff *146*
Spon End, Coventry *48, 89, 152*
Spooner, Charles *178*
steelworks 69
Stepney *50, 51*
Stoneleigh 37
street vendors 62, *63*
Suggitts Lane, Cleethorpes 60, *61*
Summerhill, Blaenau Ffestiniog 174, *175*
Sutherland, Graham 46

Tabernacl chapel, Blaenau Ffestiniog *121*
Tal-y-Waenydd *166*
Tan-y-grisiau 23, *36*, 55, *185*; Terrace *169*
Telfer, Pete 198, *199*
Telford, Thomas 127
Temple Street library, Newport 98, *99*
terraced houses *9, 10, 31*, 62, 75, 76, 77, *90-92, 96-97, 110, 169, 174*
theatre 57, *103*
Thoreau, Henry David 23–25
Tickler's Preserves, Grimsby *162*
town halls 99
towns 50 –73
tramways *128, 174, 178-79, 181*
transport 126-41
Tremadog church *116*, 117
Turner, J.M. 46
Tŷ Uncorn 75, *78–83*

Usk, River 33, 138
Uskside ironworks *163*
Uwchllaw'r FFynnon 28, *76, 192-93*

Van Gogh, Vincent 47
ventilation grille 48
viaducts 6, 7, *128*
Vyrnwy, Lake *133*

Walden Pond 23–25
Wallis, Alfred 47
Ward and Austin architects 17
Ward, Neville 19
watch making *150, 152, 155*
Watkins, William *186*
water supply *133*
weaver's: houses *74, 75, 89, 155*; shop *7*
weaving 23, 37–38, *40*, 41, *155-61*
Weedon, Harry *112*
weighbridge *70*
Welsh Brewers, Cardiff *147*
Wesley, John *123*
winding house *176*
windmills 46, 188
windows *87*
Windsor Castle Hotel, Newport *115*
Wivenhoe *60-61*
Woolwich 19, *39*; school *108*
Word in Your Eye 43, 195
workers' housing *10, 74, 75, 76, 77*
Worktown 29, 193, 198

Ynys Enlli *49*
Young Men's Christian Association (YMCA) 99, *105*

Lord Street in Snow, 1983

This atmospheric winter scene captures Lord Street in Blaenau Ffestiniog in the snow, showing the severe weather that workers' housing in north Wales had to withstand.

Pencil and watercolour, 38 x 52 cm. FHA 01/015